D0042222

To

_____

From

_____

*It's in Christ that we find out who we are and
what we are living for. Long before we first heard
of Christ ... he had his eye on us, had designs
on us for glorious living, part of the overall purpose
he is working out in everything and everyone.*

EPHESIANS 1:11 (MSG)

THE PURPOSE
DRIVEN LIFE

Journal

updated edition

WHAT ON EARTH
AM I HERE FOR?

A Guided Journal by

RICK WARREN

ZONDERVAN

ZONDERVAN.com/
AUTHOR**TRACKER**
follow your favorite authors

ZONDERVAN

The Purpose Driven® Life Journal
Copyright © 2003, 2013 by Rick Warren

Requests for information should be addressed to:

Zondervan, Grand Rapids, Michigan 49530

978-0-310-33723-2

All Scripture quotations, unless otherwise indicated, are taken from The Holy Bible, *New International Version®, NIV®*. Copyright © 1973, 1978, 1984, 2011 by Biblica, Inc.™ Used by permission. All rights reserved worldwide.

Additional Scripture versions cited in this book are identified in appendix 3, which hereby becomes a part of this copyright page.

Any Internet addresses (websites, blogs, etc.) and telephone numbers in this book are offered as a resource. They are not intended in any way to be or imply an endorsement by Zondervan, nor does Zondervan vouch for the content of these sites and numbers for the life of this book.

All rights reserved. No part of this publication may be reproduced, stored in a retrieval system, or transmitted in any form or by any means — electronic, mechanical, photocopy, recording, or any other — except for brief quotations in printed reviews, without the prior permission of the publisher.

Cover design: Brian Montes
Cover illustration: iStockphoto®
Interior illustration: iStockphoto®
Interior design: Beth Shagene

Printed in the United States of America

A Journey with Purpose

Before you were born, God planned this moment in your life. It is no accident that you have chosen to read *The Purpose Driven Life*. God longs for you to discover the life he created you to live — here on earth, and forever in eternity.

Ⓥ

As I wrote *Purpose Driven Life*, I prayed you would experience the incredible joy that comes from knowing God's purposes for your life. I admire you for your interest in this book. It shows you want to know your purpose, and God loves that. You'll learn the big picture — how all the pieces of the puzzle fit together. This perspective on life will reduce your stress, increase your satisfaction, help you make better decisions, and most importantly, prepare you for eternity.

I invite you to join me in a life-defining *40-day spiritual journey* that answers life's most important question: What on earth am I here for? The best way to reinforce your progress in fulfilling God's purposes for your life is to keep a spiritual journal. This is not a diary of events, but a record of the life lessons you don't want to forget. We remember what we record. Writing helps clarify what God is doing in your life.

If you're serious about fulfilling your life's purpose you can't be in a hurry. God isn't. So slow down and take the time to reflect, discuss what you read each day, and then journal. Allow the Scripture to speak to you.

Your life is a journey and a journey deserves a journal. You owe it to future generations to preserve the testimony of how God helped you to fulfill his purposes on earth. It is a witness that will continue long after you are in heaven.

Rick Warren

Write down for the coming generation
what the LORD has done,
so that people not yet born will praise him.
PSALM 102:18 (GNT)

WHAT ON EARTH
AM I HERE FOR?

It All Starts with God

For everything, absolutely everything,
above and below, visible and invisible, . . .
everything got started in him and finds its purpose in him.

COLOSSIANS 1:16 (MSG)

POINT TO PONDER: It's not about me.

QUESTION TO CONSIDER: How can I remind myself today that life is really about living for God, not myself?

The purpose of your life is far greater than your own personal fulfillment, your peace of mind, or even your happiness. It's far greater than your family, your career, or even your wildest dreams and ambitions.

Sat. Coffee

Psalm 97:10   2/18/17

W/ yesenia's coffee group.
I shared about the peace god
has shown me in interacting
with our Business Landlords.

There is an alternative to speculation about the meaning and purpose of life. It's *revelation.* We can turn to what God has revealed about life in his Word. The easiest way to discover the purpose of an invention is to ask the creator of it. The same is true for discovering your life's purpose: ask God.

> God's wisdom ... goes deep into the interior of his purposes....
> It's not the latest message, but more like the oldest—
> what God determined as the way to bring out his best in us.
> 1 CORINTHIANS 2:7 (MSG)

_____

_____

_____

_____

_____

_____

_____

_____

_____

_____

_____

_____

_____

_____

_____

_____

_____

_____

_____

*Father, as I begin this journey, help me to realize that building
my life around myself instead of you will only lead to emptiness
and meaninglessness. I was made by you and for you,
and I want to discover my purpose in you.*

You Are Not an Accident

"I am your Creator. You were in my care
even before you were born," says the Lord.
ISAIAH 44:2 (CEV)

POINT TO PONDER: I am not an accident.

QUESTION TO CONSIDER: Knowing that God created me for a purpose, what
areas of my personality, background, and appearance do I need to accept?

Long before you were conceived by your parents you were conceived in the
mind of God. It is not fate, nor chance, nor luck, nor coincidence that you
are breathing at this very moment. You are alive because God wanted to
create you!

_____

_____

_____

_____

_____

_____

_____

_____

_____

_____

_____

_____

O LORD, You saw me before I was born and scheduled
each day of my life before I began to breathe.
Every day was recorded in your book!
PSALM 139:16 (LB)

God made you to love you and you are his special creation.

God was thinking of you even *before* he made the world! In fact, that's why he created it! God designed this planet's environment just so we could live in it. We are the focus of his love, and the most valuable of all his creation.

———————————————————————————

———————————————————————————

———————————————————————————

———————————————————————————

———————————————————————————

———————————————————————————

———————————————————————————

———————————————————————————

———————————————————————————

———————————————————————————

———————————————————————————

———————————————————————————

———————————————————————————

———————————————————————————

———————————————————————————

———————————————————————————

———————————————————————————

———————————————————————————

———————————————————————————

———————————————————————————

———————————————————————————

———————————————————————————

———————————————————————————

Long before he laid down earth's foundations,
he had us in mind, had settled on us as the focus of his love.
EPHESIANS 1:4 (MSG)

If there was no God, then we'd all be "accidents," the result of astronomical random chance in the universe. But there *is* a God, he made you for a reason, and your life has profound meaning! We discover that meaning and purpose *only* when we make God the reference point of our lives.

_____

_____

_____

_____

_____

_____

_____

_____

_____   *God doesn't play dice.*
                                                ALBERT EINSTEIN
_____

_____

_____

_____

_____

_____

_____

_____

_____

_____

God, your plan is amazing.
Thank you that I was custom-made for a reason.
Help me to trust your wisdom in choosing my parents,
race, background, gifts, and appearance.

DAY 3

What Drives Your Life?

*You, LORD, give perfect peace to those who keep
their purpose firm and put their trust in you.*
ISAIAH 26:3 (TEV)

POINT TO PONDER: Living on purpose is the path to peace.

QUESTION TO CONSIDER: What would my family and friends say is the driving
force of my life? What do I want it to be?

Everyone's life is driven by something. Most dictionaries define the verb
drive as "to guide, to control, or to direct." Whether you are driving a car,
a nail, or a golf ball, you are guiding, controlling, and directing it at that
moment. What is the driving force in your life?

_____

_____

_____

_____

_____

_____

_____

_____

_____

_____

_____

Jesus said, "No one can serve two masters."
MATTHEW 6:24 (NLT)

Many people are driven by guilt, resentment and anger, fear, materialism, or the expectations of others. This journal will help you to live a *purpose-driven* life — guided, controlled, and directed by God's purposes. Nothing matters more than knowing God's purposes for your life.

We are all products of our past but we don't have to be prisoners of it. God's purpose is not limited by your past. He can turn a murderer (Moses) into a leader, a coward (Gideon) into a courageous hero, and he can do amazing things with the rest of your life.

There are five great benefits of living a purpose-driven life:

- Knowing your purpose gives your life meaning.
- Knowing your purpose simplifies your life.
- Knowing your purpose focuses your life.
- Knowing your purpose motivates your life, and ...
- Fulfilling your purpose will create an eternal legacy.

_____

_____

_____

_____

_____

_____

_____

_____

_____

_____

_____

_____

_____

_____

_____

_____

_____

_____

_____

_____

Everyone wants to be remembered when they're gone. Ultimately, what matters most will not be what others say about your life but what *God* says about you. How will you answer God when he asks, *"What did you do with my Son, Jesus Christ?"* and *"What did you do with what I gave you?"*

_____

_____

_____

_____

_____

_____

Remember, we will
_____
all stand before the
_____
judgment seat of God...
Yes, each of us
will give a personal
_____
account to God.
_____
ROMANS 14:10, 12 (NLT)

_____

_____

_____

_____

_____

_____

_____

_____

Father, I don't want my life to be driven
by anything but love for you. Help me to center my life
on your plan and purpose for me,
and not worry about the expectations of others.

DAY 4

Made to Last Forever

This world is fading away, along with everything that people crave. But anyone who does what pleases God will live forever.
1 JOHN 2:17 (NLT)

POINT TO PONDER: There is more to life than just here and now.

QUESTION TO CONSIDER: Since everything has eternal consequences, what is one thing I should stop doing and one thing I should start doing today?

You have an inborn instinct that longs for immortality. This is because God designed you, in his image, to live for eternity. The reason we feel we should live forever is because God wired our brains with that desire! God has planted eternity in the human heart (Ecclesiastes 3:11 NLT).

_____

_____

_____

_____

_____

_____

_____

_____

_____

_____

_____

_____

Surely God would not have created such a being as man to exist only for a day! No, no, man was made for immortality.
ABRAHAM LINCOLN

How you relate to God now on earth will determine where you spend eternity. If you develop a relationship of love and trust in God through his Son, Jesus Christ, you'll spend the rest of eternity with him. When you live in light of eternity, your values change. You use your time and money more wisely. You place a higher premium on relationships and character instead of fame or wealth or achievements, or even fun. Your priorities are reordered. Keeping up with trends, fashions, and popular values, just doesn't matter as much anymore.

_____

_____

_____

_____

_____

_____

_____

_____

_____

_____

_____

_____

_____

_____

_____

_____

_____

_____

Paul wrote, "I once thought these things were valuable, but now I consider them worthless because of what Christ has done."

PHILIPPIANS 3:7 (NLT)

[God's] plans endure forever;
his purposes last eternally.
PSALM 33:11 (TEV)

God has a purpose for your life on earth but it doesn't end here. His plan involves far more than the few decades you'll spend on this planet. It's more than "the opportunity of a lifetime"; God offers you an opportunity *beyond* your lifetime.

_____

_____

_____

_____

_____

_____

_____

_____

_____

_____

_____

_____

_____

_____

_____

_____

_____

_____

_____

God, open my eyes to see that there are eternal consequences
in even the smallest choices of my life. Remind me to look past
what is temporary and focus on what will last forever.
Teach me to live in light of eternity.

Seeing Life from God's View

If you are faithful in little things,
you will be faithful in large ones.
LUKE 16:10 (NLT)

POINT TO PONDER: Life is a test and a trust.

QUESTION TO CONSIDER: What has happened to me recently that I now realize was a test from God? What are the greatest trusts God has entrusted to me?

The Bible says life is a test, life is a trust, and life is a temporary assignment. These ideas are the foundation of purpose-driven living. To fulfill the purposes God created you for, you'll have to challenge conventional wisdom and replace it with the biblical metaphors of life.

_____

_____

_____

_____

_____

_____

_____

_____

_____

_____

Do not conform yourselves to the standards of this world,
but let God transform you inwardly by a complete change
of your mind. Then you will be able to know the will of God.
ROMANS 12:2 (TEV)

When you understand that life is a test, you realize that *nothing* is insignificant in your life. Even the smallest incident has significance for your character. *Every* day is an important day, and every second is a growth opportunity to develop character, to demonstrate love, or to depend on God. Some tests seem enormous and overwhelming while others you don't even notice. But all of them have eternal implications.

Blessed are those who endure when they are tested.
When they pass the test, they will receive the crown of life
that God has promised to those who love him.
JAMES 1:12 (GWT)

Never forget that everything in your life really belongs to God: your home, children, job — everything. You're just a caretaker, a trustee, a steward of it all. It's your privilege to enjoy it but it's also your responsibility to faithfully use it the way God wants it used.

Our culture says, "If you don't own it, you won't take care of it." But Christians live by a higher standard: "Because *God* owns it, I must take the best care of it that I can."

Those who are trusted with something valuable must show they are worthy of that trust.
1 CORINTHIANS 4:2 (NCV)

At the end of your life on earth you'll be evaluated and rewarded according to how well you handled what God entrusted to you. That means *everything* you do, even simple daily chores, has eternal implications. If you treat everything as a *trust,* God promises three rewards in eternity. First, you'll be given God's *affirmation:* He'll say, "Good job! Well done!" Next, you'll receive a *promotion* and be given greater responsibility in eternity: "I will put you in charge of many things." Then, you'll be honored with a *celebration:* "Come and share your Master's happiness."

_____

_____

_____

_____

_____

_____

_____

_____

_____

_____

_____

_____

_____

_____

_____

_____

_____

_____

_____

Gracious God, give me the wisdom to see life as you see it.
Help me to pass the test of character you place before me and
to treat everything you give me as a sacred trust.
You own it all; I just get to use it while I'm on earth.

Life Is a Temporary Assignment

We fix our eyes not on what is seen, but on what is unseen,
since what is seen is temporary, but what is unseen is eternal.

2 CORINTHIANS 4:18 (NIV)

POINT TO PONDER: This world is not my home.

QUESTION TO CONSIDER: Since life on earth is just a temporary assignment, how should that change the way I live today?

To make the best use of your life you must never forget two truths: First, compared to eternity, life is brief. Second, earth is only a temporary residence for you. You won't be here long, so don't get too attached. Ask God to help you see life on earth as he sees it. With all the fascinating attractions, mesmerizing media, and enjoyable experiences available today, it's easy to forget that the pursuit of happiness is not what life is about. Only as we remember that life is a test, a trust, and a temporary assignment will the appeal of these things lose their grip on our lives.

_____

_____

_____

_____

_____

_____

_____

_____

_____

The things we see now are here today, gone tomorrow.
But the things we can't see now will last forever.

2 CORINTHIANS 4:18 (MSG)

In God's eyes, the greatest heroes of faith are not those who achieve prosperity, success, and power in this life, but those who treat this life as a temporary assignment and serve faithfully expecting their promised reward in eternity.

_____

_____

_____

_____

_____

_____

_____

_____

_____

_____

_____

_____

_____

_____

_____

_____

_____

_____

_____

_____

_____

_____

This world is fading away, along with everything that people crave. But anyone who does what pleases God will live forever.
1 JOHN 2:17 (NLT)

We fix our eyes not on what is seen, but on what is unseen,
since what is seen is temporary, but what is unseen is eternal.
2 CORINTHIANS 4:18 (NIV)

When life gets tough, when you're overwhelmed with doubt, when you see evil prospering, or when you wonder if living for Christ is worth the effort, remember that you are not home yet. At death you won't leave home — you'll *go* home.

_____

_____

_____

_____

_____

_____

_____

_____

_____

_____

_____

_____

_____

_____

_____

_____

_____

_____

Lord, help me remember that there is more to life than
just here and now. Remind me to live like a temporary resident,
not getting too attached to the things of this world
because they are not what is going to last.

DAY 7

The Reason for Everything

"For everything comes from God alone.
Everything lives by his power,
and everything is for his glory."
ROMANS 11:36 (LB)

POINT TO PONDER: It's all for him.

QUESTION TO CONSIDER: How in my daily routine could I become more aware of God's glory around me?

The ultimate goal of the universe is to show the glory of God. It is the reason for everything that exists, including you. God made it *all* for his glory. Living for God's glory is the greatest achievement you can accomplish with your life. God says, *"They are my own people, and I created them to bring me glory"* (Isaiah 43:7 TEV), so it ought to be the supreme goal of our lives.

_____

_____

_____

_____

_____

_____

_____

_____

_____

_____

_____

_____

_____

Jesus honored God by fulfilling his purpose on earth. We bring God glory the same way.

There are many ways to bring glory to God but they can be summarized in God's five purposes for your life.

- We bring God glory by worshiping him.
- We bring God glory by loving other believers.
- We bring God glory by becoming like Christ.
- We bring God glory by serving others with our gifts.
- We bring God glory by telling others about him.

_____

_____

_____

_____

_____

_____

_____

_____

_____

_____

_____

_____

_____

_____

_____

_____

_____

_____

_____

_____

_____

There are three secrets about the glory of God that most people miss. First, when you trust Christ with your life, God puts his glory *in you!* The second secret is that the more you focus on living for God's glory, the more you will be filled with joy! The third secret is that if you've committed your life to Jesus, one day you are going to share in God's glory! God repeatedly promises that if we live for his glory on earth, we'll share his glory for eternity!

_____

_____

_____

_____

_____

_____

_____

_____

_____

_____

_____

_____

_____

_____

_____

_____

_____

_____

_____

_____

_____

_____

_____

Will you live for your own goals, comfort, and pleasure, or will you live the rest of your life for God's glory, knowing that he's promised eternal rewards? You may hesitate, wondering if you'll have strength to live for God. Don't worry. Jesus will give you everything you need to live for him if you'll just make the choice to do it.

> *Everything that goes into a life of pleasing God*
> *has been miraculously given to us by getting to know,*
> *personally and intimately, the One who invited us to God.*
>
> 2 PETER 1:3 (MSG)

Wonderful God, it is my deepest desire to bring you glory.
Help me to see your glory all around me today.
Nothing would exist without you. It's all for your glory!

YOU WERE PLANNED FOR GOD'S PLEASURE

Planned for God's Pleasure

The LORD takes pleasure in his people.

PSALM 149:4 (TEV)

POINT TO PONDER: I was planned for God's pleasure.

QUESTION TO CONSIDER: What could I start doing today as if I was doing it for Jesus?

Bringing pleasure to God is called worship. It is the first and primary purpose of your life. Anything you do that brings pleasure to God is an act of worship. Like a diamond, worship is *multifaceted*. Worship is a lifestyle.

_____

_____

_____

_____

_____

_____

_____

_____

_____

_____

_____

_____

_____

_____

O Lord, . . . you created all things,
and they exist because
you created what you pleased..

REVELATION 4:11 (NLT)

We worship for God's benefit. When we worship, our goal is to bring pleasure to God, not ourselves. Worship isn't for you. It's for God. Of course, there are many benefits to worship, but we don't worship to please ourselves. Our motive is to bring glory and pleasure to our Creator.

_____

_____

_____

_____

_____

_____

_____

_____

_____

_____

_____

_____

_____

_____

_____

_____

_____

_____

_____

_____

_____

The LORD is pleased only with those
who worship him and trust his love.
PSALM 147:11 (CEV)

*"Take your everyday, ordinary life—your sleeping,
eating, going-to-work, and walking-around life—
and place it before God as an offering."*
ROMANS 12:1 (MSG)

Worship is not what you do with your lips; it's what you do with your *life*. All the singing, praying, and praising is worthless if it doesn't lead to personal change and commitment. You can't be a spectator in worship. Passive worship is an oxymoron. Real worship is offering yourself to live for God's pleasure.

_____

_____

_____

_____

_____

_____

_____

_____

_____

_____

_____

_____

_____

_____

_____

_____

_____

*Father, thank you for creating me for your own pleasure!
I would not even exist if you hadn't chosen to make me.
If I don't get anything else done today, help me to know
and love you a little bit more before I go to sleep tonight.
Help me to develop a lifestyle of worship.*

DAY 9

What Makes God Smile?

The LORD is pleased only with those
who worship him and trust his love.
PSALM 147:11 (CEV)

POINT TO PONDER: God smiles when I trust him.

QUESTION TO CONSIDER: Since God knows what's best, in what areas of my life do I need to trust him more?

Since bringing pleasure to God is the first purpose of your life, your most important task is to discover how to do that. Fortunately, the Bible gives us a clear example of a life that gives pleasure to God. The man's name was Noah. From his life, we learn the five acts of worship that make God smile.

- God smiles when we love him supremely.
- God smiles when we trust him completely.
- God smiles when we obey him wholeheartedly.
- God smiles when we praise and thank him.
- God smiles when we fulfill his purposes.

_____

_____

_____

_____

_____

_____

_____

_____

_____

_____

_____

_____

This is what God wants most from you: a relationship! God deeply loves you and *desires* your love in return. He *longs* for you to know him and spend time with him. He delights in you. Building a relationship with God, and learning to love and be loved by him, should be the greatest objective of your life. Nothing else even comes close in importance.

Jesus replied, " 'Love the Lord your God with all your heart and with all your soul and with all your mind.' This is the first and greatest commandment."

MATTHEW 22:37 – 38 (NIV)

We please God by what we do
and not only by what we believe.
JAMES 2:24 (CEV)

God's Word is very clear that you can't earn your salvation. It is only by grace, not your effort. But as a child of God you can bring pleasure to your heavenly Father through obedience. Search through your Bible and make a list of the small obediences that God says bring him pleasure. All of these can be acts of worship. Why is obedience so pleasing to God? Because it proves you really love him.

_____

_____

_____

_____

_____

_____

_____

_____

_____

_____

_____

_____

_____

_____

_____

_____

Jesus said, "If you love me,
you will obey my commandments."
JOHN 14:15 (TEV)

*The LORD looks down from heaven on all mankind to see if
there are any who are wise, who want to please God.*
PSALM 14:2 (LB)

When you live in light of eternity, the question changes from "How much pleasure am I getting out of life?" to "How much pleasure is God getting out of my life?" God is looking for people like Noah in the 21st century — people willing to live for the pleasure of God. This lifestyle of worship is the only wise, sensible way to live.

_____

_____

_____

_____

_____

_____   *Figure out what
                                          will please Christ,
_____   and then do it.*
                                          EPHESIANS 5:10 (MSG)
_____

_____

_____

_____

_____

_____

_____

_____

_____

_____

_____

*Dear God, I want my life to bring a smile to your face.
Empower me to love you supremely, trust you completely
and obey you wholeheartedly today.*

The Heart of Worship

Give yourselves to God ...
surrender your whole being to him
to be used for righteous purposes.
ROMANS 6:13 (TEV)

POINT TO PONDER: The heart of worship is surrender.

QUESTION TO CONSIDER: What area of my life am I holding back from God? What am I afraid of?

Surrendering to God is the heart of worship. True worship — bringing God pleasure — happens when you give yourself completely to God. Offering yourself to God is what worship is all about. This act of personal surrender is called many things: consecration, making Jesus Lord, taking up your cross, dying to self, yielding to the Spirit. What matters is that you do it, not what you call it. God wants your life. All of it. 95% is not enough.

_____

_____

_____

_____

_____

_____

_____

_____

_____

_____

_____

_____

_____

_____

Trust is an essential ingredient to surrender. You won't surrender to God unless you trust him, but you can't trust him until you know him better. Fear keeps us from surrendering but *love casts out all fear.* The more you realize how much God loves you, the easier surrender becomes. God is a Lover and a Liberator, and surrendering brings freedom, not bondage. When we completely surrender ourselves to Jesus, we discover that he is not a tyrant but a Savior; not a boss, but a brother; not a dictator, but a friend.

Surrendering is best demonstrated in obedience; cooperating with your Creator. You say, *"Yes, Lord"* to whatever he asks of you. The supreme example of self-surrender is Jesus. The night before his crucifixion Jesus surrendered himself to God's plan. He prayed, *"Father, everything is possible for you. Please take this cup of suffering away from me. Yet I want your will to be done, not mine"* (Mark 14:36 NLT). Genuine surrender says, "Father, if this problem, pain, sickness, or circumstance is needed to fulfill your purpose and glory in my life or in another's, please *don't* take it away!"

_____

_____

_____

_____

_____

_____

_____

_____

_____

_____

_____

_____

_____

_____

_____

_____

_____

_____

_____

_____

_____

_____

Give yourselves completely to God.
JAMES 4:7 (NCV)

If God is going to do his deepest work in you, it will begin with surrender. So give it all to God; your past regrets, your present problems, your future ambitions, your fears, dreams, weaknesses, habits, hurts, and hang-ups. Put Christ in the driver's seat of your life and take your hands off the steering wheel. Don't be afraid; nothing under his control can ever be out of control. Mastered by Christ, you can handle anything.

_____

_____

_____

_____

_____

_____ *The heart of*
worship is
_____ *surrender.*

_____

_____

_____

_____

_____

_____

_____

_____

_____

_____

Dear loving Father, when I think of all you've done for me,
I want to surrender all my life to your will.
I want to give up my need to control things and trust in you instead.
Help me to hold back nothing from you today.

Becoming Best Friends with God

*Friendship with God is reserved
for those who reverence him.*
PSALM 25:14 (LB)

POINT TO PONDER: God wants to be my best friend.

QUESTION TO CONSIDER: How could I remind myself to talk to God more often throughout my day?

Adam and Eve enjoyed an intimate friendship with God. Unhindered by guilt or fear, they delighted in God and he delighted in them. We were made to live in the environment of God's continual presence, but after the Fall that ideal relationship was lost. Yet because Jesus secured our salvation and left his Holy Spirit in us, we all can become friends of God now. *Since our friendship with God was restored by the death of his Son while we were still his enemies, we will certainly be saved through the life of his Son* (Romans 5:10 NLT).

_____

_____

_____

_____

_____

_____

_____

_____

*Now we can rejoice in our wonderful new relationship
with God because our Lord Jesus Christ has made us
friends of God.*
ROMANS 5:11 (NLT)

Friendship with God is built by sharing *all* your life experiences with him. God wants to be more than an appointment in your schedule. He wants to be included in *every* activity, every conversation, every problem, and even every thought. Friendships are built on shared experiences — celebrations, tragedies, challenges, routines, highs and lows. You build a friendship with God the same way: by spending time together interacting, talking, listening, and going through a variety of circumstances together.

_____

_____

_____

_____

_____

_____

_____

_____

_____

_____

_____

_____

_____

_____

_____

_____

_____

_____

_____

It's impossible to be God's friend apart from *knowing what he says.* You can't love God unless you know him, and you can't know him without knowing his Word. While you cannot spend all day studying the Bible, you can *think* about it throughout the day, recalling verses you've read or memorized, and mulling them over in your mind. The reason God considered Job and David close friends was because they valued and esteemed his Word above everything else, and they thought about it continually throughout the day.

_____

_____

Oh, how I love your law!
I meditate on it all day long.
PSALM 119:97 (NIV)

A third way to build a friendship with God is by being honest with him. God expects honesty, not perfection. If perfection was a requirement, none of us could ever be friends of God. None of God's friends in the Bible were perfect. We're only his friends by grace. Jesus is still the *"friend of ... sinners"* (Matthew 11:19). In the Bible, the friends of God were honest about their feelings. God, however, didn't seem to be bothered by this frankness; in fact, he encouraged it.

_____

_____

_____

_____

_____

_____

Knowing and loving God is
_____   *our greatest privilege, and*
                                    being known and loved
_____   *is God's greatest pleasure.*

_____

_____

_____

_____

_____

_____

_____

_____

_____

Jesus, forgive me for being too busy to develop
a friendship with you. I want to develop a running dialogue,
a continual conversation with you throughout the day.

DAY 12

Developing Your Friendship with God

Come close to God,
and God will come close to you.
JAMES 4:8 (NLT)

POINT TO PONDER: I'm as close to God as I choose to be.

QUESTION TO CONSIDER: What choices will I make today in order to grow closer to God?

To instruct us in candid honesty, God gave us the book of Psalms — a worship manual, full of ranting, raving, doubts, fears, resentments, and deep passions combined with thanksgiving, praise, and statements of faith. Every possible emotion is catalogued in the Psalms. When you read the emotional confessions of David and others, realize this is how God wants you to worship him — holding back nothing of what you feel.

_____

_____

_____

_____

_____

_____

_____

_____

_____

_____

He offers his friendship to the godly.
PROVERBS 3:32 (NLT)

You build a friendship with God by caring about what God cares about. This is what friends do — they care about what is important to the other person. The more you become God's friend, the more you will care about the things God cares about, grieve over the things God grieves over, and rejoice over the things that bring pleasure to God. What does God care about most? He wants all his lost children found! That's the whole reason Jesus came to earth. The dearest thing to the heart of God is the death of his Son. The second dearest thing is when his children share that news with others.

Your love means more than life to me.

PSALM 63:3 (CEV)

You build a friendship with God by desiring it more than anything else. Intimate friendship with God is a choice, not an accident. You must intentionally seek it. Do you really want it — more than anything? You may have been passionate about God in the past but you've lost that desire. To reignite your passion for God, start asking him to give it to you, and keep on asking until you have it. Pray this throughout your day:

Dear Jesus, more than anything else, I want to get to know you intimately.

Jesus, I want a deeper relationship with you.
Help me to be completely honest with my feelings and my faults.
Nothing matters more than my relationship to you.

DAY 13

Worship That Pleases God

Love the Lord your God with all your heart
and with all your soul and with all your mind
and with all your strength.

MARK 12:30 (NIV)

POINT TO PONDER: God wants *all* of me.

QUESTION TO CONSIDER: Which is more pleasing to God right now — my public worship or my private worship? What will I do about this?

God-pleasing worship is based on Scripture. Real worship is rooted in the Word; it's based on truth, not our imagination. God-pleasing worship is also from the heart. Made in God's image, you are a spirit that resides in a body, and God designed your spirit to communicate with him. Worship is our spirit responding to God's Spirit.

_____

_____

_____

_____

_____

_____

_____

_____

_____

_____

_____

Let us be grateful and worship God in a way
that will please him, with reverence and awe.

HEBREWS 12:28 (TEV)

God-pleasing worship is thoughtful. Reading Scripture in different translations and paraphrases will expand your expressions of worship. Try praising God without using the words *praise, hallelujah, thanks,* or *amen.* Make a list of synonyms and use fresh words like *admire, respect, value, revere, honor, and appreciate.* Be *specific.* You'd rather receive two specific compliments than 20 vague generalities. So would God. Another idea is to make a list of the different names of God and focus on them. God's names are not arbitrary; they tell us about different aspects of his character. And God commands us to praise his name.

_____

_____

_____

_____

_____

_____

_____

_____

_____

_____

_____

_____

_____

_____

_____

_____

_____

_____

_____

_____

God-pleasing worship is sacrificial. Real worship costs. One thing worship costs us is our self-centeredness. You cannot exalt God and yourself at the same time. You don't worship to be seen by others or to please yourself. You deliberately shift the focus off yourself. When Jesus said, *"Love God with all your strength"* he pointed out that worship takes effort and energy. It is not always convenient or comfortable, and sometimes worship is a sheer act of the will — a willing sacrifice.

_____

_____

_____

_____

_____

_____

_____

_____

_____

_____

_____

_____

_____

_____

_____

_____

_____

_____

_____

I will not offer to the Lord my God sacrifices
that have cost me nothing.
2 SAMUEL 24:24 (TEV)

Praise him from sunrise to sunset!
PSALM 113:3 (LB)

God-pleasing worship is continual. Praise should be the first activity when you open your eyes in the morning and when you close them at night. Worship is not a part of your life, it is your life, and every activity can be transformed into an act of worship when you do it for the praise, glory, and pleasure of God.

_____

_____

Worship is the first purpose of your life. It is our greatest responsibility, our highest privilege, and it should take priority over everything else.

_____

_____

_____

_____

_____

_____

_____

_____

_____

_____

_____

_____

_____

Father, I want to bring you pleasure today by loving you
with all my heart and mind and soul and strength.
Help me to identify and develop the sacred pathway
that fits how you created me to know you.

When God Seems Distant

God has said, "I will never leave you;
I will never abandon you."
HEBREWS 13:5 (TEV)

POINT TO PONDER: God is real, no matter how I feel.

QUESTION TO CONSIDER: How do I intend to stay focused on God even when he feels distant?

Friendships are often tested by separation and silence. In your friendship with God, you won't always *feel* close to him. The deepest level of worship is praising God in spite of pain, thanking God during a trial, trusting God when tempted, surrendering while suffering, and loving God when he seems distant.

_____

_____

_____

_____

_____

_____

_____

_____

_____

_____

Any relationship involves times of closeness and times of
distance, and in a relationship with God, no matter how intimate,
the pendulum will swing from one side to the other.
PHILIP YANCEY

God has promised repeatedly, "I will *never* leave you nor forsake you" (Hebrews 13:5 PH). But God has *not* promised, "You will always *feel* my presence." In fact, God admits that sometimes he hides his face from us. There will be times when God appears to be *MIA,* missing-in-action, in your life. It's a normal part of the testing and maturing of your friendship with God. *Every* single Christian goes through it at least once, and usually several times. It's painful and disconcerting, but it is absolutely vital for the development of your faith.

Faith develops when you don't feel anything.

God's omnipresence and the manifestation of his presence are two different things. One is a fact; the other is often a feeling. God is always present, even when you're unaware of him, and his presence is too profound to be measured by mere emotion. Yes, he wants you to sense his presence, but he's more concerned that you *trust* him than that you *feel* him. Faith, not feelings, pleases God.

_____

_____

_____

_____

_____

_____

_____

_____

_____

_____

_____

_____

_____

_____

_____

_____

_____

_____

_____

_____

_____

_____

_____

Naked I came from my mother's womb,
and naked I will depart. The LORD gave and the LORD
has taken away; may the name of the LORD be praised.
JOB 1:21 (NIV)

How do you praise God when you don't understand what's happening in your life and God is silent? You do what Job did.

- Tell God exactly how you feel.
- Focus on who God is — his unchanging nature.
- Trust God to keep his promises.
- Remember what God has already done for you.

_____

_____

_____

_____

When you feel abandoned
by God, yet continue to   _____
trust him in spite of your
feelings, you worship God   _____
in the deepest way.
                                   _____

                                   _____

_____

_____

_____

_____

_____

_____

_____

God, when I don't hear your voice or feel your presence,
help me to seek you, not a feeling. Then help me remember
your promise that you will never leave me nor forsake me.

YOU WERE FORMED FOR GOD'S FAMILY

Formed for God's Family

God decided in advance to adopt us into his own
family by bringing us to himself through Jesus Christ.

EPHESIANS 1:5 (NLT)

POINT TO PONDER: I was formed for God's family.

QUESTION TO CONSIDER: How can I start treating other believers like members of my own family? What could I do today?

God wants a family, and he created you to be a part of it. This is God's second purpose for your life, which he planned before you were born. The entire Bible is the story of God building a family who will love him, honor him, and reign with him forever.

_____

_____

_____

_____

_____

_____

_____

_____

_____

_____

_____

_____

_____

_____

_____

_____

The moment you were spiritually born into God's family, you were given some astounding birthday gifts: the family name, the family likeness, family privileges, family intimate access, and the family inheritance! As children in God's family we are given: *the riches ... of [his] grace ... kindness ... patience ... glory ... wisdom ... power ... and mercy* (Ephesians 1:7; Romans 2:4; 9:23; 11:33; Ephesians 3:16; 2:4). We also inherit eternal life. What an inheritance! You are far richer than you realize.

And we have a priceless inheritance—an inheritance
that is kept in heaven for you, pure and undefiled,
beyond the reach of change and decay.
1 PETER 1:4 (NLT)

*Jesus and the people he makes holy all belong
to the same family. That is why he isn't ashamed
to call them his brothers and sisters.*
HEBREWS 2:11 (CEV)

Because Jesus makes you holy, God is proud of you. Being included in God's family is the highest honor, the greatest privilege you and I will ever receive. Nothing else comes close. Why not pause right now and thank God that he included you?

_____

_____

_____

_____

_____

_____

_____

_____

_____

_____

_____

_____

_____

_____

_____

_____

_____

*Thank you, dear God, that you made me
to be a part of your family forever!
What a privilege it is to be included.
Help me to never take your church for granted.*

What Matters Most

The entire law is fulfilled in keeping this one command:
"Love your neighbor as yourself."
GALATIANS 5:14 (NIV)

POINT TO PONDER: Life is all about love.

QUESTION TO CONSIDER: Honestly, are relationships the top priority in my life? How could I insure that they are?

Since God is love, the most important lesson he wants you to learn on earth is how to love. It is in loving that we are most like him, so love is the foundation of every command he's given us. God wants us to love everyone, but he is particularly concerned that we learn to love others in his family. This is the second purpose of your life and it's called fellowship. Jesus said our love for each other is our greatest witness to the world.

_____

_____

_____

_____

_____

_____

_____

_____

_____

_____

_____

No matter what I say, what I believe,
and what I do, I'm bankrupt without love.
1 CORINTHIANS 13:3 (MSG)

The best use of your life is love. It should be your top priority, your primary objective, your greatest ambition. Love is not a good part of your life; it's *the most* important part. Relationships must have first place in your life above everything else. Why? God gives us three reasons: life without love is really worthless; love will last forever; and love is what you'll be evaluated on in eternity. Jesus summarized what matters most to God in two statements: love God and love people.

_____

_____

_____

_____

_____

_____

_____

_____

_____

_____

_____

_____

_____

_____

_____

_____

_____

_____

_____

_____

_____

Let love be your greatest aim.

1 CORINTHIANS 14:1 (LB)

Our love should not be just words and talk;
it must be true love, which shows itself in action.
1 JOHN 3:18 (TEV)

The best expression of love is time. Time is your most precious gift because you only have a set amount of it. You can make more money but you can't make more time. When you give someone your time, you are giving them a portion of your life that you'll never get back. Your time is your life. That's why the greatest gift you can give someone is your time. Whenever you give your time you're making a sacrifice, and sacrifice is the essence of love.

_____

_____

_____

_____

_____

_____

_____

_____

_____

_____

_____

_____

_____

_____

_____

_____

_____

_____

_____

_____

_____

_____

Whenever we have the opportunity,
we should do good to everyone.
GALATIANS 6:10 (NLT)

The best time to love is now. You don't know how long you'll have the opportunity to express love. Circumstances change. People die. Children grow up. You have no guarantee of tomorrow. If you want to express love you'd better do it now.

_____

_____

_____

_____

_____

_____

_____

_____

_____

_____

_____

_____

_____

_____

_____

_____

_____

_____

Father, help me to remember that life is all about love.
Today I will take the time to love the people you place in my path.
Remind me that loving others is never a waste of time.
Teach me to love those who seem unlovable and give them
what they need, not what they deserve.

A Place to Belong

In Christ we, though many, form one body,
and each member belongs to all the others.
ROMANS 12:5 (NIV)

POINT TO PONDER: I'm called to belong, not just believe.

QUESTION TO CONSIDER: Does my level of involvement in my church demonstrate that I love and am committed to God's family?

Even in the perfect, sinless environment of Eden God said, "It is not good for the man to be alone" (Genesis 2:18). We're created for community, fashioned for fellowship, formed for a family, and none of us can fulfill God's purposes by ourselves. While your relationship to Christ is personal, God never intends it to be private. In God's family you're connected to every other believer, and we'll belong to each other for eternity. *You are members of God's very own family, citizens of God's country, and you belong in God's household with every other Christian* (Ephesians 2:19 LB).

_____

_____

_____

_____

_____

_____

_____

_____

_____

_____

_____

_____

To Paul, being a member of the church meant being a vital organ of a living body, an indispensable, interconnected part of the body of Christ. We need to recover and practice the biblical meaning of membership. The church is a body, not a building; an organism, not an organization. You were created for a specific role in Christ's body, but you'll miss this second purpose of your life if you're not attached to a living, local church. We discover our role in life through our relationships with others and significance comes, not from within yourself, but from being a part of Christ's body.

_____
_____
_____
_____
_____
_____
_____
_____
_____
_____
_____
_____
_____
_____
_____
_____
_____
_____
_____
_____

The local church is the classroom for learning how to get along in God's family. It is a lab for practicing love. Only in regular contact with ordinary, imperfect believers can we learn real fellowship, and experience the New Testament truth of being *connected* and *dependent* on each other. True fellowship is being as committed to each other as we are to Jesus Christ. And when we come together in love as a church family from different backgrounds, race, and social status it is a witness to the world.

_____

_____

_____

_____

_____

_____

_____

_____

_____

_____

_____

_____

_____

_____

_____

_____

*Your love for one another will prove
to the world that you are my disciples.*
JOHN 13:35 (NLT)

You need a purpose to live for, people to live with, principles to live by, a profession to live out, and power to live on. God intends for his church to provide these. In fact, the five purposes of the church are identical to God's five purposes for your life. Worship helps you *focus on God;* fellowship helps you *face life's problems;* discipleship helps *fortify your faith;* ministry helps *find your talents;* evangelism helps *fulfill your mission.* There is nothing else on earth like the church!

_____

_____

_____

_____

_____

_____

_____

_____

_____

_____

_____

_____

_____

_____

_____

_____

_____

_____

*Dear God, help me to remember that whenever I become careless
about fellowship with other believers, I'm moving away from you.
Forgive me for the times I've gotten detached from your Body, the church.
Help me to stay connected and committed,
and love your church the way you do.*

Experiencing Life Together

*Share each other's burdens, and
in this way obey the law of Christ.*
GALATIANS 6:2 (NLT)

POINT TO PONDER: I need others in my life.

QUESTION TO CONSIDER: What one step could I take today to connect with another believer at a more genuine, heart-to-heart level?

God intends for us to weave our lives together. The Bible calls this *fellowship*. Fellowship is *experiencing life together*. That includes unselfish loving, honest sharing, practical serving, sacrificial giving, sympathetic comforting, and all the other *"one another"* commands found in the New Testament. When it comes to fellowship size matters; *smaller is better*. Every Christian needs to be involved in a small group within your church, whether it is a home fellowship group, Sunday school class, or a small Bible study. This is where real community takes place.

We experience authenticity in genuine fellowship. Fellowship is not superficial, surface-level interaction. It's genuine, sometimes gut-level sharing. It happens when people honestly share themselves — their thoughts, feeling, doubts, fears, strengths, and weaknesses. Of course, this is quite a risk, requiring both courage and humility. It means facing our fear of exposure, rejection, and being hurt again. Why would anyone take such a risk? Because it is the only way to grow spiritually.

_____

_____

_____

_____

_____

_____

_____

_____

_____

_____

_____

_____

_____

_____

_____

_____

_____

_____

Make this your common practice:
Confess your sins to each other and pray for each other
so that you can live together whole and healed.
JAMES 5:16 (MSG)

We experience mutuality and sympathy in genuine fellowship. Mutuality is the art of giving and receiving. It's depending on each other. Mutuality is the heart of fellowship: building reciprocal relationships, sharing responsibilities, and helping each other. Sympathy is understanding and affirming someone's feelings. It meets two fundamental human needs: the need to be understood and the need to have your feelings validated. Sympathy says, "I know what you're going through and what you feel is neither strange nor crazy." Sympathy is entering in and sharing the pain.

_____

_____

_____

_____

_____

_____

_____

_____

_____

_____

_____

_____

_____

_____

_____

_____

_____

_____

_____

_____

_____

_____

How wonderful it is, how pleasant,
for God's people to live together in harmony!
PSALM 133:1 (TEV)

We experience mercy in genuine fellowship. It's a place of grace, where your mistakes aren't rubbed in but rubbed out. Fellowship and forgiveness go together. Because we're all imperfect, sinful people we hurt each other — sometimes intentionally and sometimes unintentionally. That means we need massive amounts of mercy and grace in order to live together. We need to offer it and receive it. Fellowship happens when mercy wins over justice.

_____

_____

_____

_____

_____

_____

_____

_____

_____

_____

_____

_____

_____

_____

_____

Father, I want you to use me to help build real fellowship in my church.
Help me to be authentic with others and not wear a mask.
Teach me to show sympathy to those who are hurting and
offer mercy to those who have stumbled.

Cultivating Community

We understand what love is when we realize
that Christ gave his life for us. That means
we must give our lives for other believers.
1 JOHN 3:16 (GWT)

POINT TO PONDER: Community requires commitment.

QUESTION TO CONSIDER: How could I help cultivate the characteristics
of real community in my small group and church?

To help build genuine fellowship in your church or small group, you must
make the effort to do five things: be honest, be humble, be courteous,
respect confidentiality, and have frequent, regular contact with others.
Relationships take time and effort, but the benefits far outweigh the costs
and Jesus expects us to love each other the way he loves us.

_____

_____

_____

_____

_____

_____

_____

_____

_____

_____

You can develop a healthy, robust community that
lives right with God and enjoy its results only if you
do the hard work of getting along with each other,
treating each other with dignity and honor.
JAMES 3:18 (MSG)

Make the effort to be humble and courteous. Humility is the oil that smoothes and soothes relationships. The Bible says in 1 Peter 5:5, *Clothe yourselves with humility toward one another, because, "God opposes the proud but shows favor to the humble."* Courtesy is showing respect for our differences, and being considerate even when we disagree with each other. Paul told Titus that there should be *"no insults, no fights. God's people should be bighearted and courteous."* We all have peculiar quirks and annoying traits. But community has nothing to do with compatibility. The basis for our fellowship is our relationship to God; we're family.

_____

_____

_____

_____

_____

_____

_____

_____

_____

_____

_____

_____

_____

_____

_____

_____

_____

_____

_____

_____

Let us not give up the habit of meeting together,
as some are doing. Instead, let us encourage one another.
HEBREWS 10:25 (TEV)

Deep fellowship is built with confidentiality. Only in the safe environment
of warm acceptance and trusted confidentiality will people open up and
share their deepest hurts, needs, and mistakes. Confidentiality means
that what is shared in your group needs to stay in your group. Also, deep
fellowship is built with frequency. You must have frequent, regular contact
with your group in order to build genuine fellowship with them. Fellowship
requires an investment of your time. Real fellowship takes effort.

_____

_____

_____

_____

_____

_____

_____

_____

_____

_____

_____

_____

_____

_____

God, help me not to settle
for superficial relationships with other believers.
Help me connect to a small group of believers in my church
where I can learn what real love is all about.

Restoring Broken Fellowship

Do everything possible on your part
to live in peace with everybody.
ROMANS 12:18 (TEV)

POINT TO PONDER: Relationships are always worth restoring.

QUESTION TO CONSIDER: Who do I need to restore a broken relationship with today?

Jesus said, "God blesses those who work for peace, for they will be called the children of God" (Matthew 5:9 NLT). If you want God's blessing on your life, and you want to be known as a child of God, you must learn to be a peacemaker. Since you were formed to be a part of God's family and the second purpose of your life on earth is to learn how to love and relate to others, peacemaking is one of the most important skills you can develop. *[God] has restored our relationship with him through Christ, and has given us this ministry of restoring relationships* (2 Corinthians 5:18 GWT).

_____

_____

_____

_____

_____

_____

_____

_____

_____

_____

_____

Peacemaking is not avoiding conflict. Jesus, the Prince of Peace, was never afraid of conflict. On occasion, he *provoked* it for the good of everyone. Sometimes we need to avoid conflict, sometimes we need to create it, and sometimes we need to resolve it. That's why we must pray for the Holy Spirit's continual guidance. Peacemaking is also not *appeasement.* Always giving in, acting like a doormat, and allowing others to always run over you is not what Jesus had in mind. Christ refused to back down on many issues, standing his ground in the face of evil opposition.

_____

_____

_____

_____

_____

_____

_____

_____

_____

_____

_____

_____

_____

_____

_____

_____

_____

_____

_____

_____

God ... called us to settle
our relationships with each other.
2 CORINTHIANS 5:18 (MSG)

Here are seven biblical steps to restoring fellowship:

- Talk to God before talking to the person.
- Always take the initiative.
- Sympathize with their feelings.
- Confess my part of the conflict.
- Attack the problem, not the person.
- Cooperate as much as possible.
- Emphasize reconciliation, not resolution.

_____

_____

_____

_____

_____

_____

_____

_____

_____

_____

_____

_____

_____

_____

_____

_____

_____

Who do you need to contact as a result of this chapter? With whom do you need to restore fellowship? Don't delay another second. Pause right now and talk to God about that person. Then pick up the phone and begin the process. These seven steps are simple but they are not easy. It takes a lot of effort to restore a relationship. That's why Peter urged, *"Search for peace, and work to maintain it"* (1 Peter 3:11 NLT). But when you work for peace you're doing what God would do. That's why God calls peacemakers his children.

---

*Father, give me clear vision to see how to best restore
a broken relationship. I need wisdom, humility, love, and courage
to do the right thing and take the first step to restoration.*

Protecting Your Church

Let us concentrate on the things
which make for harmony and the growth
of one another's character.
ROMANS 14:19 (PH)

POINT TO PONDER: It's my responsibility to protect the unity of my church.

QUESTION TO CONSIDER: What am I personally doing to protect the unity in my church family right now?

God loves unity. God desires us to experience *oneness* and harmony with each other. The Trinity is unified and God wants us to be unified, too. Our heavenly Father, like every parent, enjoys watching his children get along with each other. Jesus, in his final moments before being arrested, prayed passionately for our unity. And the Holy Spirit is the one who unites us in love.

_____

_____

_____

The group of believers
were united in their
hearts and spirit …
In fact, they shared
everything.
ACTS 4:32 (NCV)

Nothing is more valuable to God than his church. He paid the highest price for it, and it is worth protecting. Part of your responsibility as a believer is to protect the unity where you fellowship. You need to think of yourself as an agent of unity, commissioned by Jesus Christ to promote and preserve the fellowship among believers.

_____

_____

_____

_____

_____

_____

_____

_____

_____

_____

_____

_____

_____

_____

_____

_____

_____

_____

_____

_____

_____

_____

Make every effort to keep the unity
of the Spirit through the bond of peace.
EPHESIANS 4:3 (NIV)

Here are some ways you can be an agent of unity:

- Focus on what we share in common, not our differences.
- Be realistic in your expectations.
- Choose to encourage rather than criticize.
- Refuse to listen to gossip.
- Support your pastor and leaders.
- Practice God's method for conflict resolution:

  If a fellow believer hurts you, go and tell him — work it out between the two of you. If he listens, you've made a friend. If he won't listen, take one or two others along so that the presence of witnesses will keep things honest, and try again. If he still won't listen, tell the church (Matthew 18:15 – 17 MSG).

_____

_____

_____

_____

_____

_____

_____

_____

_____

_____

_____

_____

_____

_____

_____

_____

_____

_____

*Don't be concerned for your own good
but for the good of others.*
1 CORINTHIANS 10:24 (NLT)

I challenge you to accept your responsibility to protect and promote the unity of your church. Put your full effort into it and God will be pleased. It will not always be easy. Sometimes you'll have to do what's best for the body, not yourself, showing preference to others. That's one reason God puts us in a church family — to learn unselfishness. In community we learn to say "we" instead of "I," and "our" instead of "mine."

_____

_____

_____

_____

_____

_____

_____

_____

_____

_____

_____

_____

_____

_____

_____

_____

*Father, I need your wisdom to act in ways
that protect the unity of your church.
Help me to squelch gossip and instead be an encourager.
I want to be a unifier, not a divider.*

PURPOSE #3

YOU WERE CREATED
TO BECOME LIKE CHRIST

Created to Become Like Christ

*The Lord—who is the Spirit—makes us more and more
like him as we are changed into his glorious image.*

2 CORINTHIANS 3:18 (NLT)

POINT TO PONDER: I was created to become like Christ.

QUESTION TO CONSIDER: In what area of my life do I need to ask for the Spirit's power to be like Christ today?

From the very beginning, God's plan has been to make you like his Son, Jesus. This is your destiny, and the third purpose of your life. What does the full image and likeness of God look like? It looks like Jesus Christ! On earth, God's ultimate goal for your life is not comfort, but Christlike character.

_____

_____

_____

_____

_____

_____

_____

_____

_____

_____

_____

*God knew what he was doing from the very beginning.
He decided from the outset to shape the lives of those who
love him along the same lines as the life of his Son.... We
see the original and intended shape of our lives there in him.*

ROMANS 8:29 (MSG)

Only the Holy Spirit has the supernatural power to make the changes God wants to make in our lives. This process is called *sanctification.* It's not a matter of trying really hard to be like Jesus, but trusting and listening to his Spirit, who lives inside us. However, the Holy Spirit releases his power the *moment* you take a step of faith. He waits for you to act first. God also uses his Word, his people, and circumstances to mold us. God's Word provides the truth we need to grow, God's people provide the support we need to grow, and circumstances provide the environment to practice Christlikeness.

_____

_____

_____

_____

_____

_____

_____

_____

_____

_____

_____

_____

_____

_____

_____

_____

_____

_____

_____

_____

He has not yet shown us what we will be like
when Christ appears. But we do know that we will
be like him, for we will see him as he really is.
1 JOHN 3:2 (NLT)

Becoming like Christ is a long, slow process of growth. Spiritual maturity is neither instant nor automatic; it is a gradual, progressive development that will take the rest of your life. Our transformation into Christlikeness will be completed when we get to heaven or when Jesus returns. When we are finally able to see Jesus perfectly, we'll become perfectly like him. Jesus wants to make us like himself before he takes us to heaven. This is our greatest privilege, our immediate responsibility, and our ultimate destiny.

_____

_____

_____

_____

_____

_____

_____

_____

_____

_____

_____

_____

_____

_____

_____

_____

_____

Jesus, I want to learn to think like you, speak like you,
feel what you feel, and act the way you would act.
Please use your Words and your Spirit to make me like you.

How We Grow

Let God transform you inwardly by a complete change
of your mind. Then you will be able to know the will of God
—what is good and is pleasing to him and is perfect.
ROMANS 12:2 (TEV)

POINT TO PONDER: It's never too late to start growing.

QUESTION TO CONSIDER: What is one area where I need to stop thinking my way and start thinking God's way?

Your heavenly Father's goal is for you to mature and develop the characteristics of Jesus Christ, living a life of love and humble service. Spiritual growth is not automatic. It takes an intentional commitment. You must *want* to grow, *decide* to grow, *make an effort* to grow, and *persist* in growing. Discipleship — the process of becoming like Christ — always begins with a decision.

_____

_____

_____

_____

_____

_____

_____

_____

_____

_____

_____

Once you decide to get serious about becoming like Christ, you must begin to act in new ways. You'll need to let go of some old routines, develop some new habits, and intentionally change the way you think.

There are two parts of spiritual growth: *"work out"* and *"work in."* The *"work out"* is your responsibility and the *"work in"* is God's role. Spiritual growth is a collaborative effort between you and the Holy Spirit.

_____

_____

_____

_____

_____

_____

_____

_____

_____

_____

_____

_____

_____

_____

_____

_____

_____

_____

Continue to work out your salvation with fear and trembling,
for it is God who works in you to will and to act in order
to fulfill his good purpose.

PHILIPPIANS 2:12 – 13 (NIV)

Let God transform you into a new person
by changing the way you think.
ROMANS 12:2 (NLT)

Your first step in spiritual growth is to start changing the way you think. The way you *think* determines the way you *feel,* and the way you feel influences the way you *act.* To be like Christ you must develop the mind of Christ. The New Testament calls this mental shift *"repentance,"* which in Greek literally means *"to change your mind."* To repent means to change the way you think — about God, yourself, sin, other people, life, your future, and everything else. You adopt Christ's outlook and perspective on life.

When I became a man, I put the
ways of childhood behind me.
1 CORINTHIANS 13:11 (NIV)

There are two parts to thinking like Jesus. The first half of this mental shift is to stop thinking *immature* thoughts, which are self-centered and self-seeking. The second half is to start thinking *maturely*, which focuses on others, not yourself. Thinking of others is the heart of Christlikeness, and the goal of spiritual growth. This kind of thinking is unnatural, countercultural, and rare. The only way we will learn to think this way is by filling our minds with the Word of God.

_____

_____

_____

_____

_____

_____

_____

_____

_____

_____

_____

_____

_____

_____

_____

_____

_____

Dear Father, I want to cooperate with your Spirit's work in my life today.
Help me to listen to your teachings and develop my mind like Christ's.

Transformed by Truth

[Jesus said,] "If ye continue in my word,
then are ye my disciples indeed;
and ye shall know the truth,
and the truth shall make you free."
JOHN 8:31 – 32 (KJV)

POINT TO PONDER: The truth transforms me.

QUESTION TO CONSIDER: What has God already told me to do in his Word
that I haven't started doing yet?

The Spirit of God uses the Word of God to make us like the Son of God.
To become like Jesus, we must fill our lives with his Word. God's Word is
the essential spiritual nourishment you *must* have to fulfill your purpose.
The Bible is called our milk, bread, solid food, and sweet dessert. This four-
course meal is the Sprit's menu for spiritual strength and growth. To be a
healthy disciple of Jesus, feeding on God's Word must be your first priority.
Jesus called it *"abiding."*

_____

_____

_____

_____

_____

_____

_____

_____

_____

People do not live by bread alone, but by every word
that comes from the mouth of God.
MATTHEW 4:4 (NLT)

Abiding in God's Word is a lifestyle that includes three daily decisions. First, I must accept its authority. The most important task you can do today is settle this issue of what's going to be the ultimate authority for your life. Decide that regardless of culture, tradition, reason, or emotion you choose the Bible as your final authority. Determine to first ask, "What does the Bible say?" when making decisions. Settle it in your mind that when God says to do something you'll trust God's Word and do it whether or not it makes sense, or if you feel like doing it.

Every word of God is flawless.
PROVERBS 30:5 (NIV)

To abide in God's Word I must assimilate its truth. There are five ways to do this:

1. **Receive** God's Word — listen and accept it with an open, receptive attitude.
2. **Read** the Bible daily — it will keep you in range of God's voice.
3. **Research** or study the Bible, asking questions about the text and writing down your insights.
4. **Remember** it — memorizing Bible verses will help you resist temptation, make wise decisions, build confidence, offer good advice, and share your faith with others.
5. **Reflect** daily on Scripture — there is no other habit that can do more to make you more like Jesus.

_____

_____

_____

_____

_____

_____

_____

_____

_____

_____

_____

_____

_____

_____

_____

_____

_____

*Jesus said, "Now that you know these things,
you will be blessed if you do them."*
JOHN 13:17 (NIV)

To abide in God's Word I must apply its principles. I must become *"a doer
of the Word"* (James 1:22 KJV). God's blessing comes from obeying the
truth, not just knowing it. The best way to become a "doer of the Word"
is to always write out an action step as a result of your reading or studying
or reflecting on God's Word. Develop the habit of writing down exactly
what you intend to do.

_____

_____

_____

_____

_____

_____   *The Bible was not given
to increase our knowledge
but to change our lives.*
D. L. MOODY

_____

_____

_____

_____

_____

_____

_____

_____

_____

_____

*Father, I thank you for your powerful, life-changing Word.
I want my mind to be saturated with Scripture.
Help me to build my life on your truth.*

DAY 25

Transformed by Trouble

We know that in all things God works for the good of those who love him, who have been called according to his purpose.
ROMANS 8:28 (NIV)

POINT TO PONDER: There is a purpose behind every problem.

QUESTION TO CONSIDER: What problem in my life has caused the greatest growth in me?

God has a purpose behind every problem. You should expect four kinds of problems in life:

- **Trials** are designed by God to draw us closer to him and build our character. **Temptations** are designed by the Devil to draw us away from God and destroy our character.
- **Trespasses** are hurts caused by the sins of others.
- **Troubles** are usually, but not always, the consequences of our own sinful choices.

_____

_____

_____

_____

_____

_____

_____

_____

_____

_____

_____

When you face a problem, try to determine the source first. If the trouble is your own fault, you should **repent** of it. If it is a temptation from Satan, you should **resist** it. If it is a trespass against you by others you need to **release** it through forgiveness. But if the problem is a trial from God, you need to **relax** and trust God in it. Regardless of the source, none of your problems could happen without God's permission. Everything that happens in the life of a child of God is *Father-filtered*, and he intends to use it for good.

---

*For our light and momentary troubles are achieving
for us an eternal glory that far outweighs them all.*
2 CORINTHIANS 4:17 (NIV)

Everything that God allows to happen in your life is permitted for one great, eternal purpose: to conform your character to the image of Christ. It is for your growth and God's glory, and it is a plan guaranteed to succeed. It will be completed when you get to heaven. The Bible says Jesus *"learned obedience through suffering"* (Heb 5:8 KJV). We grow the same way, and Jesus is our model. *We go through exactly what Christ goes through. If we go through the hard times with him, then we're certainly going to go through the good times with him* (Romans 8:17 MSG).

_____

_____

_____

_____

_____

_____

_____

_____

_____

_____

_____

_____

_____

_____

_____

_____

_____

Dear God of all comfort, help me to remember that there is
a loving purpose behind every problem that you allow in my life.
Teach me to respond to the difficulties the way Jesus would.
Cultivate my character through the circumstances of life.
Help me to trust your purpose in my pain.

Growing Through Temptation

*God blesses those who patiently endure testing
and temptation. Afterward they will receive the crown
of life that God has promised to those who love him.*

JAMES 1:12 (NLT)

POINT TO PONDER: Every temptation is an opportunity to do good.

QUESTION TO CONSIDER: What Christlike character quality could I develop
by defeating the most common temptation I face?

To have the fruit of the Spirit is to be like Christ. How then does the Holy
Spirit produce his fruit in your life? Instantly? No. Fruit matures and ripens
slowly. God develops the fruit of the Spirit in your life by allowing you
to experience circumstances where you're tempted to express the exact
opposite quality! Character development always involves a choice, and
temptation provides that opportunity. Every time you defeat a temptation,
you become more like Jesus!

Overcoming temptation today

1. Refuse to be intimidated. Temptation is a sign that Satan hates you, not a sign of weakness or worldliness. It is also a normal part of being human and living in a fallen world. Don't be surprised or shocked or discouraged by it. Be realistic about the inevitability of temptation; you'll never be able to avoid it completely. The Bible says, *When* you're tempted ... not *if*. It is not a sin to be tempted. Jesus was tempted, yet he never sinned. It is not sin unless you give in to temptation, and that is a choice.

_____

_____

_____

_____

_____

_____

_____

_____

_____

_____

_____

_____

_____

_____

_____

_____

_____

_____

_____

_____

_____

_____

_____

2. Recognize your pattern of temptation and be prepared for it. There are certain situations that make you more vulnerable to temptation than others. These situations are unique to your weaknesses and you need to identify them because Satan surely knows them! He knows *exactly* what trips you up and he is constantly working to get you into those circumstances. You should identify your typical pattern of temptation and then prepare to avoid those situations as much as possible. The Bible tells us repeatedly to anticipate and be ready to face temptation. Paul wrote, *Don't give the Devil a chance* (Ephesians 4:27 TEV). Wise planning reduces temptation.

3. Request God's help. The Bible guarantees that our cry for help will be heard because Jesus is sympathetic to our struggle. He faced the same temptations we do. God's love is everlasting and his patience endures forever. If you have to cry out for God's help 200 times a day to defeat a particular temptation he'll still be eager to give mercy and grace.

> *But the Holy Spirit produces this kind of fruit in our lives: love, joy, peace, patience, kindness, goodness, faithfulness, gentleness, and self-control.*
> GALATIANS 5:22 – 23 (NLT)

_____

_____

_____

_____

_____

_____

_____

_____

_____

_____

_____

_____

_____

_____

_____

_____

_____

_____

Wonderful Father, thank you for the gift of choice.
Help me to remember that temptation is always an opportunity
to do the right thing. Today I choose your will for my life.

Defeating Temptation

God is faithful.
He will not allow the temptation
to be more than you can stand.
When you are tempted, he will show
you a way out so that you can endure.
1 CORINTHIANS 10:13 (NLT)

POINT TO PONDER: There's always a way out.

QUESTION TO CONSIDER: Who could I ask to be a spiritual partner to help me defeat a persistent temptation by praying for me?

4. Refocus your attention on something else. Ignoring a temptation is far more effective than fighting it. Once your mind is on something else, the temptation loses its power. So when temptation calls you on the phone, don't argue with it; just drop the receiver. To reduce temptation, keep your mind occupied with God's Word and other good thoughts. You defeat bad thoughts by thinking of something better. This is the principle of *replacement.* You overcome evil with good.

_____

_____

_____

_____

_____

_____

_____

_____

_____

_____

5. Reveal your struggle to a godly friend or support group. If you're losing the battle against a persistent bad habit, an addiction, or a temptation, and you're stuck in a repeating cycle of *good intention-failure-guilt,* you will not get better on your own! You need the help of others. Some temptations are *only* overcome with the help of a partner who prays for you, encourages you, and holds you accountable. God's plan for your growth and freedom includes other Christians. Authentic, honest fellowship is the antidote to your lonely struggle against those sins that won't budge. God says it is the only way you're going to break free.

_____

_____

_____

_____

_____

_____

_____

_____

_____

_____

_____

_____

_____

_____

_____

_____

_____

_____

_____

_____

_____

6. Resist the Devil. Paul tells us to, *"Put on salvation as your helmet, and take the sword of the Spirit, which is the word of God"* (Ephesians 6:17 NLT). First, you must accept God's salvation. You won't be able to say no to the Devil unless you've said yes to Christ. Without Christ, we're defenseless against the Devil, but with *the helmet of salvation* our minds are protected by God. Second, you must use the Word of God as your weapon against Satan. Jesus modeled this when he was tempted in the wilderness. Every time Satan suggested a temptation, Jesus countered by quoting Scripture. There is power in God's Word.

_____

_____

_____

_____

_____

_____

_____

_____

_____

_____

_____

_____

_____

_____

_____

_____

_____

_____

_____

_____

7. Realize your vulnerability. God warns us to never get cocky and overconfident; that is the recipe for disaster. We must never let down our guard and think we're beyond temptation. Don't carelessly place yourself in tempting situations. Avoid them. Remember that it is easier to stay out of temptation than to get out of it. Every time you stand up to a temptation you become more like Jesus.

> *When people are tempted and still continue strong,*
> *they should be happy. After they have proved their faith,*
> *God will reward them with life forever.*
> JAMES 1:12 (NCV)

_____

_____

_____

_____

_____

_____

_____

_____

_____

_____

_____

_____

_____

_____

_____

Father, I need your grace
in defeating the persistent temptations in my life.
Give me the courage to share my struggle with a friend
who can hold me accountable and give me support.

It Takes Time

God began doing a good work in you,
and I am sure he will continue it until
it is finished when Jesus Christ comes again.

PHILIPPIANS 1:6 (NCV)

POINT TO PONDER: There are no shortcuts to maturity.

QUESTION TO CONSIDER: In what area of my spiritual growth do I need to be patient and persistent?

Spiritual growth, like physical growth, takes time. While we worry about *how fast* we grow, God is concerned about *how strong* we grow. God views our lives *from* and *for* eternity so he is never in a hurry. Discipleship is the process of conforming to Christ. Christlikeness is the destination where you'll eventually arrive, but your journey will last a lifetime. So far we've seen that this journey involves *believing* (through worship), *belonging* (through fellowship), and includes *becoming* (through discipleship). Every day God wants you to become a little more like him.

_____

_____

_____

_____

_____

_____

_____

_____

_____

_____

Why does spiritual growth take so long? We are slow learners. We quickly forget God's lessons and revert to our old behavior. We have a lot to unlearn. The Bible calls this *"taking off the old self"* and *"putting on the new self."* We are afraid to humbly face the truth about ourselves. Only as God is allowed to shine the light of his truth on our faults can we begin to work on them. Growth is often painful and scary. Every change involves a loss of some kind. Habits take time to develop. Your habits define your character.

Everything on earth has its own time and its own season.
ECCLESIASTES 3:1 (CEV)

There's only one way to develop the habits of Christlike character: *practice* them over time! There are no *instant habits*. If you practice something over time, you get good at it. Repetition is the mother of character and skill. These character-building habits are often called *spiritual disciplines*.

_____

_____

_____

_____

_____

_____

_____

_____

_____

_____

_____

_____

_____

_____

_____

_____

_____

_____

_____

_____

_____

_____

Practice these things.
Devote your life to them so that
everyone can see your progress.
1 TIMOTHY 4:15 (GWT)

If it seems slow, do not despair, for these
things will surely come to pass. Just be patient!
They will not be overdue a single day!
HABAKKUK 2:3 (LB)

How to handle the wait: **Expect gradual improvement.** Believe God is working in your life even when you don't feel it. **Keep a journal of lessons learned.** Write down God's lessons so you can review and remember them. **Be patient with God and with yourself.** God's timetable is rarely the same as ours. **Don't get discouraged.** Remember how far you've come, not just how far you have to go.

_____

_____

_____

_____

_____

_____

_____

_____

_____

_____

_____

_____

_____

_____

_____

_____

Lord, when I get discouraged help me to see how far I've come,
not just how far I still have to go. Thank you that you will never
give up on me and will complete what you've started.

PURPOSE #4

YOU WERE SHAPED
FOR SERVING GOD

Accepting Your Assignment

We are God's handiwork, created in Christ Jesus to do good
works, which God prepared in advance for us to do.

EPHESIANS 2:10 (NIV)

POINT TO PONDER: Service is not optional.

QUESTION TO CONSIDER: What's holding me back from accepting God's call to serve him?

You are here to make a difference by serving God and others. This is God's fourth purpose for your life. Whenever you serve others, in any way, you are actually serving God, and fulfilling one of his purposes for creating you. We weren't placed on earth just to breathe, eat, take up space, and have fun. God fashioned each of us to make a unique contribution with our lives.

God redeemed you for the purpose of doing his holy work. You're not saved *by* service but you are saved *for* service. In God's kingdom, you have a place, a purpose, a role, and a function to fulfill. This gives your life great significance and value. Once saved, God intends to use you for his goals. God has a *ministry* for you in his body, and a *mission* for you in the world.

_____

_____

_____

_____

_____

_____

_____

_____

_____

_____

_____

_____

_____

_____

_____

_____

_____

_____

It is he who saved us and chose us
for his holy work, not because we deserved it
but because that was his plan.
2 TIMOTHY 1:9 (LB)

Jesus said, "Your attitude must be like my own,
for I, the Messiah, did not come to be served,
but to serve, and to give my life."
MATTHEW 20:28 (LB)

For Christians, service is not optional, something to be tacked onto our schedules if we can spare the time. It is the heart of the Christian life. Jesus came to serve and to give — and those two verbs should define your life on earth, too. Serving and giving sum up God's fourth purpose for your life.

_____

_____

_____

_____

_____

_____

_____

_____

_____

_____

_____

_____

_____

_____

_____

_____

Wonderful God, help me remember today
that I was put on earth to serve you by serving others.
Thank you for the privilege of being a part of what
you are doing through your church in the world.

Shaped for Serving God

God works through different people in different ways, but it is the same God who achieves his purposes through them all.
1 CORINTHIANS 12:6 (PH)

POINT TO PONDER: I was shaped for serving God.

QUESTION TO CONSIDER: In what way could I see myself passionately serving others and loving it?

You are God's handcrafted work of art. You are not an assembly-line product, mass-produced without thought. You are a custom-designed, one-of-a-kind, original masterpiece. God deliberately shaped and formed you to serve him in a way that makes your ministry unique. Not only did God shape you before your birth, he planned every day of your life to support his shaping process. This means nothing that happens in your life is insignificant. God uses *all of it* to mold you for your ministry to others, and shape you for your service to him.

_____

_____

_____

_____

_____

_____

_____

_____

_____

_____

How God Shapes You for Your Ministry

God never wastes anything. He would not give you abilities, interests, talents, gifts, personality, and life experiences unless he intended to use them for his glory. By identifying and understanding these factors you can discover God's will for your life. The Bible says you are *wonderfully complex*. You're a combination of many different factors. Five important factors form the acrostic "S.H.A.P.E." When God decided to create you, he determined exactly what you would need for your unique service. This custom combination of capabilities is called your Shape:

Spiritual gifts
Heart
Abilities
Personality
Experience

Spiritual gifts. God gives every believer spiritual gifts to be used in ministry. These are special God-empowered abilities for serving him. You can't earn your spiritual gifts. They are an expression of God's grace to you. Neither do you get to choose which gifts you'd like to have. God determines that. No single gift is given to everyone. Also no individual receives *all* the gifts. Your spiritual gifts were given for the benefit of others, just as other people were given gifts for your benefit. When we use our gifts together, we all benefit. This is why we're commanded to discover and develop our spiritual gifts.

_____

_____

_____

_____

_____

_____

_____

_____

_____

_____

_____

_____

_____

_____

_____

_____

_____

_____

_____

_____

_____

_____

Heart. The Bible uses the term "heart" to describe the bundle of desires, hopes, interests, ambitions, dreams, and affections that you have. Your heart represents the source of all your motivations — what you love to do and what you care about most. Your emotional heartbeat is the second key to understanding your shape for service. When you serve God from your heart, you serve with enthusiasm and effectiveness. Figure out what you love to do — that which God gave you a heart for — and then do it for his glory!

> *We are God's handiwork, created*
> *in Christ Jesus to do good works.*
> EPHESIANS 2:10 (NIV)

_____

_____

_____

_____

_____

_____

_____

_____

_____

_____

_____

_____

_____

_____

_____

_____

_____

God, you are an amazing Creator.
Thank you for all your attention to the details in my life.
Thank you for shaping me to serve you in a way that no one else can.

DAY 31

Understanding Your Shape

God has given each of you some special abilities;
be sure to use them to help each other,
passing on to others God's many kinds of blessings.
1 PETER 4:10 (LB)

POINT TO PONDER: Nobody else can be me.

QUESTION TO CONSIDER: What God-given ability or personal experience could I offer to my church?

Abilities. Your abilities are the natural talents that you were born with. Some people have a natural ability with words. Other people have natural athletic abilities, excelling in physical coordination. Still others are good at mathematics or music or mechanics.

To apply your abilities in service, you need to understand four truths:

- All of our abilities came from God.
- Every ability can be used for God's glory.
- What I'm able to do, God wants me to do.
- If I don't use them, I'll lose them.

_____

_____

_____

_____

_____

_____

_____

_____

_____

_____

Personality. God created each of us with a unique combination of personality traits. God made *introverts* and *extroverts.* He made people who love *routine* and those who love *variety.* He made some people *thinkers* and others *feelers.* Some people work best when given an individual assignment, while others work better with a team. There is no right or wrong temperament for ministry. We need all kinds of personalities to balance the church and give it flavor.

_____

_____

_____

_____

_____

_____

_____

_____

_____

_____

_____

_____

_____

_____

_____

_____

_____

_____

God works through different people in different ways,
but it is the same God who achieves
his purpose through them all.
1 CORINTHIANS 12:6 (PH)

Experiences. You have been shaped by your experiences in life, most of which were beyond your control. God allowed them for his purpose of molding you. In determining your shape for serving God there are at least six kinds of experiences you should examine from your past: *family* experiences, *educational* experiences, *vocational* experiences, *spiritual* experiences, *ministry* experiences, and *painful* experiences. It is this last category that God uses the most to prepare you for ministry. In fact, your *greatest* ministry will most likely come out of your greatest hurt. The very experiences that you have resented or regretted most in your life are the things God intends to use to help others!

---

*Gracious Father, I want you to use all the experiences
that have shaped my life — both good and bad — for your glory.
I am so grateful that you can even use the mistakes and failures of my life.
Help me to help others the way you've helped me.*

Using What God Gave You

Do your best to present yourself to God as one approved,
a worker who does not need to be ashamed
and who correctly handles the word of truth.

2 TIMOTHY 2:15 (NIV)

POINT TO PONDER: God deserves my best.

QUESTION TO CONSIDER: How could I make the best use of what God has given me?

The best use of your life is to serve God out of your shape. To do this you must discover, accept, enjoy, and develop the shape he's given you.

God wants you to discover your unique shape. Start finding out and clarifying what God intends for you to be and do. First, assess your gifts and abilities. Next, consider your heart and your personality. Third, examine your experiences and extract the lessons you've learned.

_____

_____

_____

_____

_____

_____

_____

_____

_____

_____

_____

_____

God wants you to accept your shape. Since God lovingly shaped you, and he knows what's best, you should gratefully accept the way he's fashioned you. Your shape was sovereignly determined by God for *his* purpose, so you shouldn't resent it or reject it. Instead you should celebrate the shape God has given only to you. Part of accepting your shape is recognizing your limitations. Nobody is good at everything and no one is called to be everything. We each have defined roles.

Since we find ourselves fashioned into all these excellently formed and marvelously functioning parts in Christ's body, let's just go ahead and be what we were made to be.
ROMANS 12:5 (MSG)

God wants you to enjoy your shape. Satan tries to rob our joy with two temptations that will prevent you from enjoying the shape God gave you: the temptation to *compare* your ministry to others, and the temptation to *conform* your ministry to the expectations of others. If you compare your shape, your ministry, or the results of your ministry with anyone else, you'll either get discouraged or you'll get full of pride. Either attitude will take you out of service and rob your job.

_____

_____

_____

_____

_____

_____

_____

_____

_____

_____

_____

_____

_____

_____

_____

_____

_____

_____

_____

*Pay careful attention to your own work, for then
you will get the satisfaction of a job well done, and
you won't need to compare yourself to anyone else.*
GALATIANS 6:4 (NLT)

God wants you to develop your shape. God expects us to make the most of what he gives us. We are to cultivate our gifts and abilities, keep our hearts aflame, grow our character and personality, and broaden our experiences so we will be increasingly more effective in our service. Remember, you're going to serve God forever in eternity. Right now, you can prepare for that ministry by practicing here on earth. Never forget that we're getting ready for eternal responsibilities and rewards. This is why, like Olympic athletes, we keep training and developing.

*Kindle afresh the gift
of God which is in you.*
2 TIMOTHY 1:6 (NASB)

*Lord, you deserve my best.
Help me to be creative in making the most of what you've given me.
I want to spend my life serving you.*

How Real Servants Act

*If you give even a cup of cold water to one of the least
of my followers, you will surely be rewarded.*
MATTHEW 10:42 (NLT)

POINT TO PONDER: I serve God by serving others.

QUESTION TO CONSIDER: Real servants make themselves available to serve; pay attention to needs; do their best with what they have; do every task with equal dedication; and are faithful to the task they have been given. Which of the five characteristics of real servants is the most challenging for me?

While knowing your shape is important for serving God, having the heart of a servant is even more important. Real servants make themselves available to serve. A servant must always be standing by for duty. Being a servant means giving up the right to control your schedule, and allowing God to interrupt it whenever he needs to. Real servants pay attention to needs. They are always on the lookout for ways to help others. When they see a need, they seize the moment to meet it. *Since we find ourselves fashioned into all these excellently formed and marvelously functioning parts in Christ's body, let's just go ahead and be what we were made to be* (Romans 12:5 MSG).

_____

_____

_____

_____

_____

_____

_____

_____

_____

Real servants do the best they can with what they have. They don't make excuses, procrastinate, or wait for better circumstances. They just do what needs to be done. God expects you to serve him with whatever you have, wherever you are, right now. Real servants do every task with equal dedication. They follow the instructions found in Colossians 3:23, *Whatever you do, work at it with all your heart, as working for the Lord, not for human masters.*

Jesus specialized in menial tasks that everyone else tried to avoid. Nothing was *beneath* him because he came to serve. It wasn't *in spite of* his greatness that he did these things, but *because* of it, and he expects us to follow his example.

Put on the apron of humility,
to serve one another.
1 PETER 5:5 (TEV)

Real servants are faithful to their ministry. They finish their tasks, fulfill their responsibilities, keep their promises, and complete their commitments. They don't leave a job half done and they don't quit when they get discouraged. They are trustworthy and dependable. Real servants maintain a low profile. They don't promote or call attention to themselves. If recognized for their service, they humbly accept it, but don't allow notoriety to distract them from their work. Real servants don't serve for the approval or applause of others. They live for an audience of One.

_____

_____

_____

_____

_____

_____

_____

_____

_____

_____

_____

_____

_____

_____

Jesus, today I make myself available
to be used by you to serve others in your name.
I want to spend my life in serving you.

DAY 34

Thinking Like a Servant

In your relationships with one another,
have the same mindset as Christ Jesus.
PHILIPPIANS 2:5 (NIV)

POINT TO PONDER: To be a servant I must think like a servant.

QUESTION TO CONSIDER: Am I usually more concerned about being served or finding ways to serve others?

To be a servant you must think like a servant. God is always more interested in *why* we do something than in what we do. Real servants are self-forgetful. They focus on others, not themselves. This is what it means to lose your life —forgetting yourself in service to others. Jesus *emptied himself by taking on the form of a servant* (Philippians 2:7 GWT). You can't be a servant if you're full of yourself. It's only when we forget ourselves that we do the things that deserve to be remembered.

_____

_____

_____

_____

_____

_____

_____

_____

_____

_____

_____

_____

Real servants think like stewards, not owners. They remember God owns it all. In the Bible, a steward was a servant entrusted to manage an estate. Servanthood and stewardship go together since God expects us to be trustworthy in both. The Bible says, *The one thing required of such servants is that they be faithful to their master* (1 Corinthians 4:2 TEV). Real servants think about their own responsibilities, not what other servants are doing. They don't compare, criticize, or compete with other servants or ministries. They're too busy doing the work God has given them. Real servants don't complain of unfairness, don't have pity-parties, and don't resent those not serving. They just trust God and keep serving.

_____

_____

_____

_____

_____

_____

_____

_____

_____

_____

_____

_____

_____

_____

_____

_____

_____

_____

Real servants base their identity in Christ. They remember they are unconditionally loved and accepted by grace so they don't have to prove their worth and they aren't threatened by lowly jobs. One of the most profound examples of serving from a secure self-image is Jesus washing the feet of his disciples. Real servants think of ministry as an opportunity, not an obligation. They enjoy helping people, meeting needs, and doing ministry. They *serve the LORD with gladness* (Psalm 100:2 KJV). God will use you if you'll begin to act and think like a servant.

_____

_____

_____

_____

_____

_____

_____

_____

_____

_____

_____

_____

_____

_____

_____

_____

_____

_____

_____

Father, help me to do what I can, with what I have, for you today.
Help me not compare or compete with others who serve you.
Help me focus solely on what you've called me to do.

God's Power in Your Weakness

Jesus said, "My grace is sufficient for you,
for my power is made perfect in weakness."

2 CORINTHIANS 12:9 (NIV)

POINT TO PONDER: God works best in weakness.

QUESTION TO CONSIDER: Am I limiting God's power in my life by trying
to hide my weaknesses? What do I need to be honest about in order
to help others?

God will use us if we allow him to work through our weaknesses. For that
to happen, we must follow the model of Paul:

Admit your weaknesses. Own up to your imperfections. Be honest about
yourself. There are two great confessions in the New Testament: The first
was Peter's, who said to Jesus, *"You are the Messiah, the Son of the living
God"* (Matthew 16:16). The second was Paul's, who said to an idolizing
crowd, *"We are only human beings like you"* (Acts 14:15 NCV).

_____

_____

_____

_____

_____

_____

_____

_____

_____

_____

_____

Be grateful for your weaknesses. Gratitude is an expression of faith in the goodness of God. It says, "God, I believe you love me, and know what's best for me." Paul gives us several reasons to be grateful for our inborn weaknesses. First, they cause us to depend on God. Our weaknesses also prevent arrogance. They encourage fellowship between believers. Most of all, our weaknesses increase our capacity for sympathy and ministry. God wants you to have a Christlike ministry on earth. That means other people are going to find healing in your wounds. Your greatest life messages and your most effective ministry will come out of your deepest hurts.

_____

_____

_____

_____

_____

_____

_____

_____

_____

_____

_____

_____

_____

_____

_____

_____

_____

_____

_____

_____

_____

_____

Honestly share your weaknesses. Ministry begins with vulnerability. Paul openly shared his failures, his feelings, his frustrations, and his fears. Of course, when you open up your life to others, you risk rejection. But the benefits are worth the risk. Vulnerability is the pathway to intimacy. This is why God wants to use your weaknesses, not just your strengths. If all people see are your strengths, they get discouraged and think, "Well, good for her, but I'll never be able to do that." But when they see God using you in spite of your weaknesses, it encourages them to think, "Maybe God could use me!"

We are weak ... yet by God's power
we will live with him in our dealing with you.
2 CORINTHIANS 13:4 (NIV)

I am with you; that is all you need.
My power shows up best in weak people.
2 CORINTHIANS 12:9 (LB)

Glory in your weaknesses. Instead of posing as self-confident and invincible, see yourself as a trophy of grace. When Satan points out your weaknesses, agree with him and fill your heart with praise for Jesus who *understands every weakness of ours* (Hebrews 4:15 CEV) and for the Holy Spirit who *helps us in our weakness* (Romans 8:26). God is never limited by our limitations.

_____

_____

_____

_____

_____

_____

_____

_____

_____

_____

_____

_____

_____

_____

_____

_____

_____

Father, use my weaknesses to show your glory.
Let my weaknesses cause me to depend on you completely.
Let my life be an example of what you can do through
ordinary people who are yielded to you.

PURPOSE #5

YOU WERE MADE
FOR A MISSION

Made for a Mission

*Jesus said, "Go and make disciples of all nations,
baptizing them in the name of the Father and of the Son
and of the Holy Spirit, and teaching them to obey
everything I have commanded you. And surely
I am with you always, to the very end of the age."*

MATTHEW 28:19–20 (NIV)

POINT TO PONDER: I was made for a mission.

QUESTION TO CONSIDER: What fears have kept me from fulfilling the mission
God made me to accomplish? What keeps me from telling others the
Good News?

Your mission — introducing people to God — is the fifth purpose of your life.
There are a number of reasons why you need to take this mission seriously.
Jesus commands us to continue his mission. The Great Commission was
not given to pastors but to *every* follower of Jesus. You are the only Christian
some people will ever know and your mission is to share Jesus with them.
Your mission is a great privilege. Although it is a profound responsibility,
it is also an incredible honor to be used by God.

Your mission is the greatest thing you can do for someone. We have the greatest news in the world and sharing it is the greatest kindness you can show to anyone. **Your mission has eternal significance.** Nothing else you do will ever matter as much as helping people establish an eternal relationship with God. **Your mission gives your life meaning.** If just one person will be in heaven because of you, your life cannot be considered a failure. **God's timetable for history's conclusion is connected to the completion of the commission we've been given.** Jesus will not return until everyone he wants to hear the Good News has heard it.

_____

_____

_____

_____

_____

_____

_____

_____

_____

_____

_____

_____

_____

_____

_____

_____

_____

_____

_____

_____

The most important thing is that I complete my mission,
the work that the Lord Jesus gave me.
ACTS 20:24 (NCV)

Completing your mission will bring glory to God. The night before he was crucified Jesus reported to his Father, *"I have brought you glory on earth by finishing the work you gave me to do"* (John 17:4). Will you be able to say that at the end of your life? **God blesses the life dedicated to his kingdom.** The secret of being blessed by God is to participate in his agenda for the world; to be a part of what he is accomplishing on earth.

_____

_____

_____

_____

_____

_____

_____

_____

_____

_____

_____

_____

_____

_____

_____

_____

_____

Father, thank you for the privilege of being a part of your plan for the world.
I want you to use me to bring others into your family for eternity.
Help me to reach even more people for Jesus.

Sharing Your Life Message

Be ready at all times to answer anyone
who asks you to explain the hope you have in you,
but do it with gentleness and respect.
1 PETER 3:15 – 16 (TEV)

POINT TO PONDER: God wants to say something to the world through me.

QUESTION TO CONSIDER: As I reflect on my personal story, who would God want me to share it with?

There are four parts to the life message God has put within you: God wants you to share your testimony. The essence of witnessing is simply reporting your personal experiences with the Lord. In a courtroom, a witness isn't expected to argue the case, prove the truth, or press for a verdict; that is the job of attorneys. Witnesses just tell what happened to them. Jesus said, *"You will be my witnesses"* (Acts 1:8), not "You must be my attorney." *Those who believe in the Son of God have the testimony of God in them* (1 John 5:10 GWT).

_____

_____

_____

_____

_____

_____

_____

_____

_____

_____

_____

God wants you to share your life lessons. The second part of your life message are the truths that God has taught you from experiences with him. These are *lessons* about God, relationships, problems, temptations, and other aspects of life. Write down the major life lessons you've learned so you can share them with others. We should be grateful Solomon did this because it gave us the books of Proverbs and Ecclesiastes, which are filled with practical lessons on living.

_____

_____

_____

_____

_____

_____

_____

_____

_____

_____

_____

_____

_____

_____

_____

_____

_____

_____

_____

A warning given by an experienced person
to someone willing to listen is more valuable than ...
jewelry made of the finest gold.
PROVERBS 25:12 (TEV)

God wants you to share your godly passions. God is a passionate God. He passionately *loves* some things and passionately *hates* other things. As you grow closer to him, he'll give you a passion for something he cares about deeply so you can be a spokesman for him in the world. It may be a passion about a problem, a purpose, a principle, or a group of people. Whatever it is, you'll feel compelled to speak up about it and do what you can to make a difference.

_____

_____

_____

_____

_____

_____

_____

_____

_____

_____

_____

_____

_____

_____

_____

_____

_____

_____

_____

_____

_____

A man's heart determines his speech.
MATTHEW 12:34 (LB)

There is no fear in love;
perfect love drives out all fear.
1 JOHN 4:18 (TEV)

God wants you to share the Good News. We must care about unbelievers because God does. Love leaves no choice. A parent will run into a burning building to save a child because their love for that child is greater than their fear. If you've been afraid to share the Good News with those around you, ask God to fill your heart with his love for them. As long as you know one person who doesn't know Christ, you must keep praying for them, serving them in love, and sharing the Good News. When you became a believer you also became God's messenger.

_____

_____

_____

_____

_____

_____

_____

_____

_____

_____

_____

_____

_____

_____

_____

_____

Lord, give me the courage to speak the unique Life Message
you've given to me. Help me to break out of my comfort zone
so you can speak through me. Put someone
in my path today so that I can share your message.

Becoming a World-Class Christian

Send us around the world with the news of your
saving power and your eternal plan for all mankind."
PSALM 67:2 (LB)

POINT TO PONDER: The Great Commission is my commission.

QUESTION TO CONSIDER: What steps could I take to prepare to go on a short-term missions experience in the next year?

World-class Christians know they were saved to serve, and made for a mission. They're eager to receive a personal assignment and excited about the privilege of being used by God. Their joy, confidence, and enthusiasm is contagious because they know they're making a difference.

_____

_____

_____

_____

_____

_____

_____

_____

_____

_____

_____

Jesus said to his followers, "Go everywhere in the world,
and tell the Good News to everyone."
MARK 16:15 (NCV)

How to Think Like a World-Class Christian

Shift from self-centered to other-centered thinking. This is a difficult mental shift because we're naturally self-absorbed. The only way we can make this paradigm switch is by a moment-by-moment dependence on God.

Don't look out only for your own interests, but take an interest in others, too.

PHILIPPIANS 2:4 (NLT)

Shift from local to global thinking. From the beginning God has wanted family members from every nation he created. The first way to start thinking globally is to begin praying for specific countries. Get a globe or map and pray for nations by name. Another way is to read and watch the news with *"Great Commission Eyes."* Wherever there is a change or conflict, you can be sure that God will use it to bring people to him. The best way is to just get up and go on a short-term mission project to another country! There's simply no substitute for hands-on, real-life experience in another culture.

_____

_____

_____

_____

_____

_____

_____

_____

_____

_____

_____

_____

_____

_____

_____

_____

_____

_____

_____

_____

_____

_____

Shift from temporal to eternal thinking. To make the most of your time on earth you must maintain an eternal perspective. This will keep you from focusing on minor issues and help you distinguish between what's urgent and what's ultimate. So much of what we waste our energy on will not matter even a year from now, much less for eternity. Don't trade your life for temporary things. What are you allowing to stand in the way of your mission? What's keeping you from being a world-class Christian? Whatever it is, let it go.

Let us strip off anything that
slows us down or holds us back.
HEBREWS 12:1 (LB)

Send us around the world with the news of your
saving power and your eternal plan for all mankind.
PSALM 67:2 (LB)

Shift from thinking of excuses to thinking of creative ways to fulfill your commission. If you want to be like Jesus, you must care about what he cares about most; you must have a heart for the whole world! You can't be satisfied with just your family and friends coming to Christ. There are over six billion people on earth and Jesus wants *all* his lost children found. The Great Commission is *your* commission, and doing your part is the secret to living a life of significance.

_____

_____

_____

_____

_____

_____

_____

_____

_____

_____

_____

_____

_____

_____

_____

_____

Father, I want to care about the whole world the way you do.
Let my heart be moved by the millions who have yet to hear the Good News
of your love. I accept the Great Commission as my commission.
Here I am, send me.

Balancing Your Life

Live life, then, with a due sense of responsibility,
not as men who do not know the meaning
and purpose of life but as those who do.

EPHESIANS 5:15 (PH)

POINT TO PONDER: Blessed are the balanced.

QUESTION TO CONSIDER: Which of the four activities will I use to stay on track and balance God's five purposes in my life?

Living with purpose takes balance and commitment. You can keep the five purposes of your life balanced and on track with four simple activities:

Expression: Talk it through with a spiritual partner or small group. The best way to *internalize* the principles of purpose-driven living is to discuss them with others in a small group setting. The Bible says, *As iron sharpens iron, so people can improve each other* (Proverbs 27:17 NCV). We learn best in community. Talk through the implications and the applications of each chapter.

_____

_____

_____

_____

_____

_____

_____

_____

_____

_____

Evaluation: Give yourself a regular spiritual checkup. The best way to *balance* the five purposes in your life is to evaluate yourself regularly. God places a high value on the habit of self-evaluation. At least five times in Scripture we're told to test and examine our own spiritual health. To do this you need to regularly check the five vital signs of worship, fellowship, character growth, ministry, and mission.

_____

_____

_____

_____

_____

_____

_____

_____

_____

_____

_____

_____

_____

_____

_____

_____

_____

_____

_____

_____

_____

*Let's take a good look at the way we're living
and reorder our lives under God.*
LAMENTATIONS 3:40 (MSG)

Reflection: Write down your progress in a journal. The best way to *reinforce* your progress in fulfilling God's purposes for your life is to keep a spiritual journal. Remember, this is not a diary of events, but a record of the life lessons you don't want to forget. We remember what we record. Writing helps clarify what God is doing in your life. Your life is a journey, and a journey deserves a journal. You owe it to future generations to preserve the testimony of how God helped you fulfill his purposes on earth. It is a witness that will continue to speak long after you're in heaven.

_____

_____

_____

_____

_____

_____

_____

_____

_____

_____

_____

_____

_____

_____

_____

_____

_____

_____

Now I want you to tell these same things
to followers who can be trusted to tell others.
2 TIMOTHY 2:2 (CEV)

Replication: Pass on what you learn to others. The best way to learn more
is to pass on what you've already learned. Those who pass on insights receive
more from God. Now that you understand the purpose of life, it's your
responsibility to carry the message to others. You probably know hundreds
of people who do not know the purpose of life. Share these truths with your
children, friends, neighbors, and those you work with.

_____

_____

_____

_____

*Passing on the purpose
of life is more than an
obligation; it's one of
life's greatest privileges.
Who will you share this
message with?*

_____

_____

_____

_____

_____

_____

_____

_____

_____

_____

_____

*Jesus, now that I know your five purposes for my life,
I ask you to help me balance them.
Don't let me overemphasize one of them to the neglect of the others.*

Living With Purpose

David ... served the purpose of God
in his own generation....
ACTS 13:36 (NASB)

POINT TO PONDER: Living with purpose is the only way to *really* live.

QUESTION TO CONSIDER: When will I take the time to write down my answers to life's five great questions? When will I put my purpose on paper?

There are many *good* things you can do with your life, but God's purposes are the five essentials you *must* do. You should commit the rest of your life to doing them. Unfortunately, it's easy to get distracted and forget what matters most. This is why it is important to develop a purpose statement for your life, one that you can review regularly. A life-purpose statement states the direction of your life, summarizes God's purposes for your life, defines success for you, expresses your shape, and clarifies your roles.

_____

_____

_____

_____

_____

_____

_____

_____

_____

_____

_____

_____

_____

Life's Five Greatest Questions

What will be the center of my life? This is the question of worship. What are you going to build your life around? You can center your life around your career, your family, or many other good things, but none is strong enough to hold you together when life starts spinning apart. You need an unshakable center.

_____

_____

_____

_____

_____

_____

_____

_____

_____

_____

_____

_____

_____

_____

_____

_____

_____

_____

_____

_____

_____

_____

_____

What will be the character of my life? This is the question of discipleship. What kind of person will you be? God is far more interested in what you *are* than what you *do.* Remember, you'll take your character into eternity, not your career.

_____

_____

_____

_____

_____

_____

_____

_____

_____

_____

_____

_____

_____

_____

_____

_____

_____

_____

_____

_____

_____

_____

_____

_____

_____

What will be the contribution of my life? This is the question of service. Knowing what your combination of spiritual gifts, heart, abilities, personality, and experiences are, what would be your best role in the family of God? Is there a specific group in the body that I am shaped to serve?

What will be the communication of my life? This is the question of your mission to unbelievers. Your mission statement should include your commitment to share your testimony and the Good News with others, the life lessons and godly passions God has given you, and the special group of people God has appointed you to reach.

_____

_____

_____

_____

_____

_____

_____

_____

_____

_____

_____

_____

_____

_____

_____

_____

_____

_____

_____

We beg you, please don't squander one bit
of this marvelous life God has given us.
2 CORINTHIANS 6:1 (MSG)

What will be the community of my life? This is the question of fellowship. How will I demonstrate my commitment to other believers and my connection to the family of God? Where will I practice the "one another" commands with other Christians? To which church family will I be joined as a functioning member? The more you grow in Christ, the more you'll love his body and want to sacrifice for it. You can begin living a purpose-driven life today.

_____

_____

_____

_____

_____

_____

_____

_____

_____

_____

_____

_____

_____

_____

_____

_____

_____

_____

Dear God, I commit the rest of my life to serving your purposes
in my generation — anywhere, anytime, anyway.
Help me to spread this message to others
so they can become what you made them to be.

Anyone who is joined to Christ is a new being;
the old is gone, the new has come.
2 CORINTHIANS 5:17 GNT

_____

_____

_____

_____

_____

_____

_____

_____

_____

_____

_____

_____

_____

_____

_____

_____

_____

_____

_____

_____

_____

_____

_____

_____

_____

_____

_____

The Envy Trap

A heart at peace gives life to the body,
but envy rots the bones.
PROVERBS 14:30 (NIV)

POINT TO PONDER: I cannot fulfill God's purpose for me if I am envying others.

QUESTION TO CONSIDER: In what areas of my life do I most often compare myself with and envy others?

While God created each of us for the same five eternal purposes, the way you fulfill those purposes — the time, place, plan, and style — is absolutely unique. God never creates clones, never copies what he's already made, and never duplicates a life plan. God only creates original masterpieces. God distinctively shaped you for a life unlike any other. Only you can be you. Only you can live the life God designed you to live. But it's also true that you cannot live a life that God designed for someone else.

_____

_____

_____

_____

_____

_____

_____

_____

_____

_____

_____

Four Harmful Effects of Envy

Envy denies your uniqueness. You have a unique thumbprint, eye print, voiceprint, footprint, and heartbeat. No one has ever been, or ever will be, like you. When you envy others, you can't see the amazing value of your own unique shape. When you stand before God someday, will he ask you why you weren't more of what he intended you to be?

We are God's masterpiece.
EPHESIANS 2:10 (NLT)

Envy divides your attention. You can't give your full concentration to becoming what God wants you to be and envy others at the same time. If you are always preoccupied watching what others do, or wishing you had what they have, you will miss seeing what God is doing in you. How will you keep your attention on God?

_____

_____

_____

_____

_____

_____

_____

_____

_____

_____

_____

_____

_____

_____

_____

_____

_____

_____

_____

_____

_____

_____

_____

_____

_____

Envy misuses your time and energy. Envy is the enemy of contentment. Envy says, "I've always got to have *more*: more money, more possessions, more power, more prestige, pleasure, and popularity." Are you in a race for more, more, more?

_____

_____

_____

_____

_____

_____

_____

_____

_____

_____

_____

_____

_____

_____

_____

_____

_____

_____

_____

_____

_____

_____

_____

_____

_____

Envy leads you to other sins. Envy *infects* everything *inside* you and *affects* everything *around* you. Whenever envy raises its head, it creates disharmony, competition, conflict, and confusion. Has envy ever caused you to lie?

_____

_____

_____

_____

_____

_____

_____

_____

_____

_____

_____

_____

_____

_____

_____

_____

_____

_____

_____

_____

_____

_____

_____

_____

Where you have envy and selfish ambition,
there you find disorder and every evil practice.
JAMES 3:16 (NIV)

Four Steps to Eradicating Envy

Stop comparing yourself to others. God has called you to be the *best you* can be, given your background, experiences, opportunities, and abilities. God doesn't judge you for talents you don't have or for opportunities you didn't get. He evaluates your faithfulness by how you lived and what you did with what you were given. In what areas of your life do you most often compare yourself with and envy others?

_____

_____

_____

_____

_____

_____

_____

_____

_____

_____

_____

_____

_____

_____

_____

_____

_____

_____

_____

_____

_____

_____

_____

_____

Celebrate God's goodness to others. Sometimes we fear that there is only a limited supply of God's goodness and grace, so if others get a bigger slice of cake, then we may not get as much. But God's grace is boundless. There is plenty to give everyone and still have an infinite amount left over! Are you ready to stop resenting God's grace to others, and learn to enjoy the successes and joys of others?

_____

_____

_____

_____

_____

_____

_____

_____

_____

_____

_____

_____

_____

_____

_____

_____

_____

_____

_____

_____

The Bible tells us to, "Rejoice with those who rejoice,
and weep with those who weep."
ROMANS 12:15 (NKJV)

Be grateful for who you are and whatever you have. Envy is based on the popular myth that having more will make you happier. But both the Bible and the testimony of millions show that is not true. Happiness is a choice. If you don't know how to be happy with what you have, you will never be happy with more. What are some ways you can make the most of your life, create beauty, and help others?

_____

_____

_____

_____

_____

_____

_____

_____

_____

_____

_____

_____

_____

_____

_____

_____

_____

_____

_____

_____

_____

Trust God when life seems unfair. One of the signs that envy has entered your heart is when you start feeling, "It's not fair! I don't have what they have!" But anytime you envy others, you are doubting that God knows what's best for you. You question his love, his justice, and even his wisdom. Are you ready to be grateful for what you've got and move on with your life?

_____

_____

_____

_____

_____

_____

_____

_____

_____

_____

_____

_____

_____

_____

_____

_____

_____

_____

_____

_____

_____

_____

_____

_____

Solomon wrote, "It is better to be satisfied with what you have than to be always wanting something else."
ECCLESIASTES 6:9 (TEV)

Solomon said, "I have also learned why people work
so hard to succeed: it is because they envy the things their
neighbors have. But it is useless. It is like chasing the wind."
ECCLESIASTES 4:4 (TEV)

_____

_____

_____

_____

_____

_____

_____

_____

_____

_____

_____

_____

_____

_____

_____

_____

_____

_____

_____

_____

_____

Dear God, thank you for creating me to be distinctively shaped,
a true masterpiece! I want to live the life you designed
for me to live. I want to fulfill your unique purpose for my life.
Help me as I turn my back on envy and move on
with the life you've given me.

The People-Pleaser Trap

Even if my father and mother abandon me,
the LORD will hold me close.

PSALM 27:10 (NLT)

POINT TO PONDER: Happiness is your choice. You don't need anyone's approval to be happy.

QUESTION TO CONSIDER: Whose approval are you living for?

There is nothing wrong with our desire to be accepted, appreciated, and approved by other people. In fact, without the affirmation of others we never actually blossom into our full potential. The dark side of the desire for approval, however, is the fear of disapproval. Fear of being criticized or rejected by others is the most common reason people get detoured from the path God planned for them.

_____

_____

_____

_____

_____

_____

_____

_____

_____

_____

_____

_____

_____

Five Dangers of People-Pleasing

People-pleasing will cause you to miss God's will for your life. God didn't create you to fulfill the expectations of others! You were planned for God's pleasure. God is always more interested in *why* you do what you do rather than where or how you do it. If you're always focused on what other people want you to be, you can't become the person God wants you to be. Have you ever done something good just to impress others or gain recognition?

People-pleasing prevents your faith from growing. Never let anyone stand in the way of your relationship with Christ. When you value anyone's opinions more than God's, you give that person power and authority that belongs only to God. When God's approval matters the most to you, the views of others lose their grip on your life. Whose opinion matters most to you?

_____

_____

_____

_____

_____

_____

_____

_____

_____

_____

_____

_____

_____

Our purpose is to please God, not people.
He alone examines the motives of our hearts.
1 THESSALONIANS 2:4 (NLT)

People-pleasing leads you to other sins. If your friends are causing you to downplay your commitment to Jesus, deny your beliefs, compromise your values, or give up on the dream God gave you, you need to find new friends! Friends who discourage your walk with God are not true friends. Can you recall times when you have caved in to peer pressure?

People-pleasing causes hypocrisy. People-pleasers wear masks and switch roles, depending on the audience. If you fall into this trap, you hide your true self, afraid that you will be rejected. Have you ever compromised your convictions in order to be socially acceptable or politically correct?

_____

_____

_____

_____

_____

_____

_____

_____

_____

_____

_____

_____

_____

_____

_____

_____

*Jesus said to the Pharisees, "You are always making
yourselves look good, but God sees what is in your heart.
The things that most people think are important
are worthless as far as God is concerned."*

LUKE 16:15 (CEV)

People-pleasing silences your life message. Until you break free from the fear of disapproval, you will be reluctant to share the powerful message God wants to communicate through you. God can't use you the way he wants to. Your testimony is stifled. Have you ever been reluctant to share your faith with others because you feared their disapproval?

_____

_____

_____

_____

_____

Do not follow the crowd in doing wrong.
EXODUS 23:2 (NIV)

_____

_____

_____

_____

_____

_____

_____

_____

_____

_____

_____

You try to get praise from each other,
but you do not try to get the praise that comes
from the only God. So how can you believe?
JOHN 5:44 (NCV)

Six Truths to Help You Resist Peer Pressure

Even God can't please everyone! Why try to do what even God can't do? It's impossible to make everyone happy at the same time. Do you try to please everyone?

You don't need anyone's approval to be happy. Happiness is a choice. What other people think of you cannot rob your happiness unless you allow it to. Are you ready to let Jesus free you from the fear of disapproval?

_____

_____

_____

_____

_____

_____

_____

_____

_____

_____

_____

_____

_____

_____

_____

_____

_____

_____

_____

If the Son sets you free,
you will be free indeed.
JOHN 8:36 (NIV)

What seems so important now is only temporary. In the light of eternity, what other people think of you right now isn't going to matter at all. In fact, it probably won't matter in just a few years. The benefits of people-pleasing never last. What benefits have you experienced from pleasing God?

You only have to please one person! If what you do pleases God, it is always the right thing to do. You can stop worrying about everyone else's reactions. This dramatically simplifies life. Is there someone whose approval matters more to you than God's?

_____

_____

_____

_____

_____

_____

_____

_____

_____

_____

_____

_____

_____

_____

_____

_____

_____

_____

The world and everything in it that people desire is passing away; but those who do the will of God live forever.
1 JOHN 2:17 (TEV)

One day you will give an account of your life to God. One day you will give an account to God. In those moments when you are tempted to water down the truth, compromise your beliefs, or deny your faith, remember that Jesus is not ashamed of you. Will Jesus be ashamed of you one day because you were ashamed of him?

Yes, each of us will give
a personal account to God.
ROMANS 14:12 (NLT)

God shapes you to be you, not somebody else. When you get to heaven, God isn't going to say, "Were you popular? Did everyone like you, and did you fulfill all their expectations?" No. God is going to say, "Did you fulfill the purpose I created you for?" What will you say?

_____

_____

_____

_____

_____

_____

_____

_____

_____

_____

_____

_____

_____

_____

_____

_____

_____

_____

_____

_____

_____

_____

_____

_____

_____

_____

Jesus said, "I don't try to please myself,
but I try to please the One who sent me.
JOHN 5:30 (NCV)

_____
_____
_____
_____
_____
_____
_____
_____
_____
_____
_____
_____
_____
_____
_____
_____
_____
_____
_____
_____
_____
_____
_____

Dear Jesus, I will not let fear of disapproval rule my life.
I will not let my human desire to be like others
or be liked by others distract me from your purpose for my life.
Help me as I strive to please you and only you.

Stop comparing yourself to others.

You are incomparable! So is everyone else. God made each of us "one of a kind." God has called you to be *the best you can be*!

> The Bible says, "When they measure themselves
> by themselves and compare themselves to themselves,
> they show how foolish they are."
> 2 CORINTHIANS 10:12 (GWT)

1. Celebrate God's goodness to others. If you would like to increase the amount of happiness you experience in life, here is one of the secrets: learn to enjoy the successes and joys of others.

> The Bible tells us to "Rejoice with those who rejoice,
> and weep with those who weep."
> ROMANS 12:15 (NKJV)

_____

_____

_____

_____

_____

_____

_____

_____

_____

_____

_____

_____

_____

_____

_____

_____

2. Be grateful for who you are and whatever you have. Happiness is a choice. Make the most of your life, create beauty, and help others.

> Solomon wrote, *"It is better to be satisfied with what you have than to be always wanting something else."*
> ECCLESIASTES 6:9 (TEV)

3. Trust God when life seems unfair. Anytime you envy others, you are doubting God's love, his justice, and even his wisdom.

_____

_____

_____

_____

_____

_____

_____

_____

_____

_____

_____

_____

_____

_____

_____

_____

_____

_____

_____

_____

_____

Why Use So Many Translations?

This book contains nearly a thousand quotations from Scripture. I have intentionally varied the Bible translations used for two important reasons. First, no matter how wonderful a translation is, it has limitations. The Bible was originally written using 11,280 Hebrew, Aramaic, and Greek words, but the typical English translation uses only around 6,000 words. Obviously, nuances and shades of meaning can be missed, so it is always helpful to compare translations.

Second, and even more important, is the fact that we often miss the full impact of familiar Bible verses, *not* because of poor translating, but simply because they have become so familiar! We *think* we know what a verse says because we have read it or heard it so many times. Then when we find it quoted in a book, we skim over it and miss the full meaning. Therefore I have deliberately used paraphrases in order to help you see God's truth in new, *fresh* ways. English-speaking people should thank God that we have so many different versions to use for devotional reading.

Also, since the verse divisions and number were not included in the Bible until 1560 A.D., I haven't always quoted the *entire* verse, but rather focused on the phrase that was appropriate. My model for this is Jesus and how he and the apostles quoted the Old Testament. They often just quoted a phrase to make a point.

Text compiled from *The Purpose Driven Life* by Rick Warren, Copyright 2002, 2011, 2012, Zondervan: Grand Rapids, MI.

Scripture marked AMP is taken from *The Amplified Bible* Copyright © 1954, 1958, 1962, 1964, 1965, 1987 by The Lockman Foundation. All rights reserved. Used by permission.

Scripture marked CEV is taken from the *Contemporary English Version*. Copyright © 1995 by American Bible Society. Used by permission.

Scripture marked GWT is taken from the *God's Word® Translation*. Copyright © 1995 by God's Word to the Nations. Published by Green Key Books. Used by permission.

Scripture marked KJV is taken from *The Holy Bible, King James Version*.

Scripture marked LB is taken from *The Living Bible*. Copyright © 1971 by Tyndale House Publishers, Inc., Wheaton, Illinois. All rights reserved.

Scripture marked MSG is taken from *The Message*. Copyright © 1993, 1994, 1995, 1996, 2000, 2001, 2002. Used by permission of NavPress Publishing Group.

Scripture marked NASB is taken from the *New American Standard Bible*. Copyright © 1960, 1962, 1963, 1968, 1971, 1972, 1973, 1975, 1977, 1995 by The Lockman Foundation. Used by permission.

Scripture marked NCV is taken from *The Holy Bible, New Century Version*, copyright © 1987, 1988, 1991 by Word Publishing, Dallas, Texas 75039. Used by permission.

Scripture marked NIV is taken from The Holy Bible, *New International Version*®, NIV®. Copyright © 1973, 1978, 1984, 2011 by Biblica, Inc.™ Used by permission. All rights reserved worldwide.

Scripture marked NJB is from *The New Jerusalem Bible*. Copyright © Doubleday & Company, Inc., 1985, New York. Used by permission.

Scripture marked NKJV is taken from the New King James Version. Copyright © 1979, 1980, 1982, by Thomas Nelson, Inc. Used by permission. All rights reserved.

Scripture marked NLT is taken from the *Holy Bible, New Living Translation*, copyright © 1996, 2004, 2007. Used by permission of Tyndale House Publishers, Inc., Wheaton, Illinois. All rights reserved.

Scripture marked NRSV is taken from the *New Revised Standard Version of the Bible*, copyright © 1989 by the Division of Christian Education of the National Council of Churches of Christ in the United States of America, and are used by permission. All rights reserved.

Scripture marked PH is taken from the *New Testament in Modern English* by J. B. Phillips, copyright © 1958 by Macmillan, New York, NY. Used by permission.

Scripture marked TEV is taken from *Today's English Version*. Copyright © American Bible Society 1966, 1971, 1976, 1992. (Also called *Good News Translation*,)

Also by Rick Warren

Available from Zondervan

The Purpose Driven® Life
The Purpose Driven® Church
Meditations on the Purpose Driven Life
Daily Inspiration for the Purpose Driven Life
Purpose Driven Life Scripture and Affirmation Keeper
Purpose Driven Life Video Curriculum
Doing Life Together — small group curriculum

Purpose Driven® Youth Ministry
Purpose Driven Youth Ministry Training Kit
Doug Fields, youth pastor at Saddleback Church

Free resources available by writing:
free@purposedrivenlife.com

A subscription to the weekly Purpose Driven Life Email Devotional
Your First Steps for Spiritual Growth booklet
Personal daily Bible reading plan
How to pray for missionaries

For those in full-time ministry
Rick Warren's Ministry Toolbox, a weekly email newsletter for pastors
toolbox@pastors.com